MW00783939

THE COMPLETE GUIDE TO REAL ESTATE OPTIONS

**What Smart Investors Need to Know —
Explained Simply**

By
Steven D. Fisher

THE COMPLETE GUIDE TO REAL ESTATE OPTIONS:
WHAT SMART INVESTORS NEED TO KNOW — EXPLAINED SIMPLY

Copyright © 2007 by Atlantic Publishing Group, Inc.
1405 SW 6th Ave. • Ocala, Florida 34471 • 800-814-1132 • 352-622-1875–Fax
Web site: www.atlantic-pub.com • E-mail: sales@atlantic-pub.com
SAN Number: 268-1250

ISBN-13: 978-1-60138-035-7   ISBN-10: 1-60138-035-6

Library of Congress Cataloging-in-Publication Data

Fisher, Steven D., 1944-
  The complete guide to real estate options : what smart investors need to know explained simply / by Steven Fisher.
     p. cm.
  Includes bibliographical references and index.
  ISBN-13: 978-1-60138-035-7 (alk. paper)
  ISBN-10: 1-60138-035-6 (alk. paper)
  1. Real estate investment--United States. 2. Option (Contract)--United States. I. Title.

  HD255.F565 2007
  332.63'24--dc22
                              2007015975

Printed on Recycled Paper

Printed in the United States

We recently lost our beloved pet "Bear," who was not only our best and dearest friend but also the "Vice President of Sunshine" here at Atlantic Publishing. He did not receive a salary but worked tirelessly 24 hours a day to please his parents. Bear was a rescue dog that turned around and showered myself, my wife Sherri, his grandparents Jean, Bob and Nancy and every person and animal he met (maybe not rabbits) with friendship and love. He made a lot of people smile every day.

We wanted you to know that a portion of the profits of this book will be donated to The Humane Society of the United States.

–Douglas & Sherri Brown

THE HUMANE SOCIETY
OF THE UNITED STATES ©

The human-animal bond is as old as human history. We cherish our animal companions for their unconditional affection and acceptance. We feel a thrill when we glimpse wild creatures in their natural habitat or in our own backyard.

Unfortunately, the human-animal bond has at times been weakened. Humans have exploited some animal species to the point of extinction.

The Humane Society of the United States makes a difference in the lives of animals here at home and worldwide. The HSUS is dedicated to creating a world where our relationship with animals is guided by compassion. We seek a truly humane society in which animals are respected for their intrinsic value, and where the human-animal bond is strong.

Want to help animals? We have plenty of suggestions. Adopt a pet from a local shelter, join The Humane Society and be a part of our work to help companion animals and wildlife. You will be funding our educational, legislative, investigative and outreach projects in the U.S. and across the globe.

Or perhaps you'd like to make a memorial donation in honor of a pet, friend or relative? You can through our Kindred Spirits program. And if you'd like to contribute in a more structured way, our Planned Giving Office has suggestions about estate planning, annuities, and even gifts of stock that avoid capital gains taxes.

Maybe you have land that you would like to preserve as a lasting habitat for wildlife. Our Wildlife Land Trust can help you. Perhaps the land you want to share is a backyard—that's enough. Our Urban Wildlife Sanctuary Program will show you how to create a habitat for your wild neighbors.

So you see, it's easy to help animals. And The HSUS is here to help.

The Humane Society of the United States
2100 L Street NW
Washington, DC 20037
202-452-1100
www.hsus.org

CONTENTS

FOREWORD 11

CHAPTER 1: INTRODUCTION 13

Advantages of the Lease Option Strategy 13

The Disadvantages of the Lease Option Strategy...........................16

CHAPTER 2: ATTITUDE IS EVERYTHING ... 19

Clear Goals 19

A Positive Mental Attitude 20

Personal Strengths...21

Self-Motivation 22

A Deep Commitment to Learning 23

Perseverance 23

Complete Commitment to Success..24

Commitment to Ethical Behavior..25

CHAPTER 3: TYPES OF LEASE OPTIONS ... 27

CHAPTER 4: GETTING STARTED 31

Sample Action Plan 35

My Action Plan 36

CHAPTER 5: SOME BASIC PRINCIPLES 37

Your Credit Rating 37

Your Current Financial Condition 45

Organize Your Office 46

CHAPTER 6: GATHERING KNOWLEDGE OF THE REAL ESTATE MARKET 49

General Market Analysis Guidelines 51

Specific Market Analysis Guidelines 61

CHAPTER 7: UNDERSTANDING REAL ESTATE MARKET PSYCHOLOGY AND VALUE .. 79

Universal Determinants of Value 80

Specific Determinants of Value 80

Three Methods of Valuation 81

The Cost Approach 81

The Income Approach 82

The Sales (Market) Comparison Approach 83

Sources of Financing 85

Information Sources 88

CHAPTER 8: FINDING PROFITABLE DEALS.... 89

Advertisements 89

Bird Dogs 90

Real Estate Investment Clubs 94

Realtors 95

Landlords.. 99

Qualified Sellers..101

A Primer on Tax-Deferred 1031 Exchange Law 107

CHAPTER 9: DUE DILIGENCE — YOUR SAFETY NET 113

Internet Searches 113

Crime Statistics 114

Demographic Information 115

Environmental Hazardous Waste 115

Property Records..115

Property Owner Names 116

Liens 117

Titles 119

Insurance Claims..119

Property Disclosure Agreements 120

CHAPTER 10: PHYSICAL INSPECTION OF THE PROPERTY 125

Finding a Building Inspector...126

What is Involved in a Building Inspection? 127

CHAPTER 11: DOING THE NUMBERS — EVALUATING PROFITABILITY 131

Factors in Evaluating Profitability 131

Appreciation 132

Cash Flow/Rental Values 133

CHAPTER 12: NEGOTIATING 137

Building Rapport 137

Negotiating Skills 141

Handling Resistance 143

Typical Forms of Resistance 145

Understand What You are Negotiating 146

Safeguard Yourself and Your Investments 149

CHAPTER 13: CLOSING 151

CHAPTER 14: ADVANCED STRATEGIES 153

Adding Protection 153

CHAPTER 15: MAXIMIZING THE APPEAL OF THE PROPERTY 157

CHAPTER 16: QUALIFYING TENANTS 161

CHAPTER 17: MANAGING TENANTS — GOOD AND BAD 165

Managing Good Tenants 165

Managing Bad Tenants 166

More Detail on the Eviction Process 168

How Evictions Work: Rules for Landlords and Property Managers 170

CHAPTER 18: RESELLING LEASE OPTIONS — MAKING YOUR PROFIT 175

Property Packaging — Selling the Sizzle and the Steak 176

Selling the Lease Option 179

Tax Considerations...180

CHAPTER 19: EXERCISING YOUR OPTION... 185

The Real Estate Settlement Procedures Act (RESPA) 189

Additional Tasks..190

CHAPTER 20: BUSINESS ADMINISTRATION ... 193

Guideline 1: Live in the computer age 193

Guideline 2: Organize your paperwork...194

Guideline 3: As you grow, delegate..196

CHAPTER 21: THINKING STRATEGICALLY... 201

The Tax Advisor...203

The Lender or Mortgage Broker..204

The Real Estate Broker and Agent 206

The Appraiser 210

The Real Estate Attorney...212

Contractors or Repairmen..212

CHAPTER 22: ACTING AS A LANDLORD 213

Landlording 214

Marketing Your Properties...218

Finding Good Tenants 223

Showing the Property 225

Moving Your Tenants In 227

Retaining Good Tenants 229

Collecting Rent 232

A Review of Eviction Procedures..235

Maintenance and Repair 237

Protecting Your Investments...238

Landlord Forms and Resources 241

The Professional Management Option..241

CHAPTER 23: TAKING ACTION..................... 247

Step 1: Review/Revise Your Action Plan....................................247

Step 2: "SWOT" Yourself..247

Step 3: Set Up Your Office 250

Step 4: Begin a Portfolio 250

Step 5: Do Your Research and Make Your Contacts.................251

Step 6: Write Proposals 251

Step 7: Build Your Team 252

Step 8: Become a Realtor 252

Step 9: Ongoing Learning and Review 252

Step 10: Lead a Balanced Life 253

Step 11: Establish a Roth IRA..256

Step 12: Form a Limited Liability Company (LLC)...................260

CONCLUSION.. 263

RESOURCES... 265

AUTHOR BIOGRAPHY..................................... 267

GLOSSARY... 269

INDEX... 285

FOREWORD

Stephanie Fox, MA,

If you believe some of the ads on television, investing in real estate is easy. With no money to invest and very little work, they tell you, you can be rich in only a few months. But, getting rich from real estate takes focus, hard work, and most importantly, knowledge.

A few lucky investors can get their rich uncle, the real estate millionaire, to teach them the ropes. For everyone else, this book can be that mentor.

As real estate markets change, property investment can be risky. Instead of buying and selling properties using significant amounts of personal money, the standard lease option can give investors a strategy that can generate income using minimum money and minimal risk. This kind of lease option (as opposed to purchase options) can be effective for both part-time and full-time investors who are willing to study the techniques and learn information they need.

What makes this book unique are the specifics. Everything you will need to know, from setting goals to scouting the right properties, and from knowing how to avoid legal and financial pitfalls to being an effective landlord are all included in remarkable detail. You can learn how to build trust to put together an effective team, what to say when you are negotiating, how to check for any one of the 28 kinds of liens that may be on a potential property, how to get and keep good renters, and when and how to sell for the greatest tax advantage. There are even sample letters to homeowners and real estate agents and rapport building exercises designed to help you reach your goals.

This is not a book you can read in an evening. This is a book that you will want to study, then return to when you take the next step or encounter a problem. It is the one comprehensive guide to owning and operating your own successful real estate investment business.

The Complete Guide to Real Estate Options by Steven Fisher will not promise you the stars, but if you are truly interested in a way to potentially make a lot of money, lease options are a very viable strategy to reaching your financial goals. While hard work is admirable, it is knowledge that gives investors the edge. Combine the two and you can become someone else's rich uncle.

Stephanie Fox, MA, is a licensed real estate agent who currently specializes in buying and selling properties in the neighborhoods of Minneapolis and St. Paul. She has worked helping her clients buy both their first homes and their first investment properties. You can contact her at:

Coldwell Banker Burnet, South Minneapolis Office,
4705 Cedar Ave. S., Minneapolis, Minnesota, 55407
612-728-2204
pfox@cbburnet.com.

1
INTRODUCTION

S imply put, a real estate lease option (also known as rent-to-own or lease-with-option) is the right to control a property without the obligation to buy it. The one who receives the option can — but is not required to — buy the property during a set period of time, which is agreed on by both parties when an option agreement is made. If the buyer does not exercise this option, it expires, and the buyer has no further obligation to the seller. Normally, a buyer has to pay an option fee. Depending on the circumstances, the fee may or not be applied to the purchase price of the property.

There are advantages and disadvantages to the option strategy in the real estate market, and these should be known from the start. In any financial transaction, knowledge keeps a person on the dry land of profitability and out of the swamp of debt.

ADVANTAGES OF THE LEASE OPTION STRATEGY

The first advantage of lease options is that they are low cost. That is, instead of coming up with the full amount to control a property, only a small percentage of cash has to be put down. Below is an example. It assumes a person wants to purchase an option on a property that is worth $500,000 and the option fee is ten percent of that price.

The Low Cost Advantage of Lease Options		
$50,000 option fee	vs.	$500,000 purchase price
(10%)	vs.	(100%)

In effect, the lease option holder has gained control of the property without the burden of ownership — the second advantage — at a low cost and achieved a third advantage — limiting the exposure to risk while preserving capital for other investments. In other words, instead of committing $500,000, only $50,000 has been paid and $450,000 has been retained for other purposes. Another way of saying this is that money has been leveraged. As stated in the companion book *The Real Estate Investor's Handbook*, control of a property can be gained for "dimes on the dollar" through the use of options. It is a good strategy for the smart investor.

A fourth advantage is the potential for a great return on an investment. Let us continue the example above to illustrate this point. Assume an annual five percent increase in property value on the $500,000 property.

Appreciation	
Purchase price =	$500,000
Annual appreciation =	x 5%
Increase in value =	$25,000
ROI (Return on Investment)	
Increase in value =	$25,000
Amount invested =	$50,000
ROI =	50%

A 50 percent return investment beats the heck out of just about any other investment.

A fifth advantage is that a person does not have to be a full-time investor to benefit from the options strategy. A job can be kept, the current lifestyle maintained, and financial security achieved through real estate investment. On the other hand, perhaps becoming a full-time investor is the goal. In that case, options are a great way to get started and establish a profitable base for future investments.

A sixth advantage relates to the objectives and mind set in the real estate market. This requires a brief explanation of two other real estate strategies:

- **Buy and Hold** — A future minded investor may want to adopt the buy and hold strategy, which involves buying a property and leasing it out. This makes the buyer the actual owner who gets all the rewards and risks of that position. With this strategy, the buyer has the option of selling at any time or holding the property for the cash flow and equity buildup for as long as desired.

- **Buy, Improve, and Hold** — This is a long-term strategy and is considered by many to be the best method of building cash flow and equity. When improvements are made to a property, higher rents can then be charged and better equity can be built up. In addition, certain improvements are classified as capital improvements by the IRS. These provide the benefit of reduction of the taxes paid on the cash flow earned from the property.

Both of these strategies work well. Simply use the one that fits the objectives. However, lease optioning does hold advantages over the other two strategies in several ways. First, it is in the nature of lease option tenants not to stay in their properties; they tend to move on. According to Matthew Chan in his book, *Turnkey Investing with Lease-Options*, tenants tend to leave within an average of three years. This is because they lack the personal or financial stability to assume conventional housing responsibilities. The benefit to the lease option holder is that when they do leave adjustments can be made to reflect changes in the marketplace; for example, charge higher up front money and higher rents, and get better option prices.

A second advantage of the lease option strategy over the other two strategies is that a profit is made in three different areas. One area is in the up front money (basically, a low down payment). For example, if three months' worth of vacancy is required and the property is moved within two months, the lease option holder comes out ahead on the turnover. This does not happen with a buy-and-hold property. Another advantage lies in the fact that not as much money has to be spent getting a lease optioned property "up to snuff" as with a buy and hold home. Cosmetic changes cost far less than with a conventional rental property. With a lease option strategy, more money is received up front and less is spent on improvements! Yet another lease option advantage lies in the fact that a higher monthly rent can be charged than with a conventional property. Also, tenants may be made responsible for basic maintenance and repair tasks. This saves money and hassle.

Finally, the option price can be set above the fair market value. This is because the lease option holder has assumed the risk and provided financing and is entitled to any appreciation of the property. Credits can also be built into the "back end" of an option. These credits are for repairs, decorating, maintenance, etc. and provide an incentive for the tenants to make repairs themselves.

Like any financial strategy, real estate lease options have their downside. Let us cover those next.

THE DISADVANTAGES OF THE LEASE OPTION STRATEGY

The first — and main — potential disadvantage of lease options is that the seller may be having financial difficulties. If this is the case, liens can be placed on the property by creditors or delinquent property taxes may need to be paid. All these issues have to be cleared up before the property can be sold. This can be a time consuming, frustrating, and aggravating process and money gets tied up in legal procedures.

However, this disadvantage can be eliminated or reduced through due diligence; that is, by doing a careful check on the seller's financial condition before agreeing to a lease option. Ideally, someone with solid credit, income, and reputation is desired. This is not always possible so a "memorandum of option" should be recorded. This document is a record against the title of the property. It lets the public know that there is an interest in the property. We will discuss the memorandum later in the book, but the purpose of this act is to prevent an unscrupulous seller from refinancing and selling the property to someone else.

Another tactic to reduce any risk in this area is to seek out sellers with considerable equity in their properties. If something bad happens to them (illness, loss of job, etc.), they have their equity to fall back on. Another disadvantage of lease options is the possibility that the property's value will not appreciate. If the property is not appraised before the option expires, the lease option holder will not be able to purchase unless he or she is willing and able to bring in the cash for the difference between the appraised value and option price. However, due diligence can, for the most part, prevent this situation. If the homework has been done and a property has been found in an area where overall values are appreciating, then it is likely the benefits of increased value will be enjoyed.

All in all, lease options are a great way to build income and future wealth as long as a person is knowledgeable and performs due diligence. But there is an important quality needed to achieve maximum success in the real estate market — the proper attitude, which is the subject of the next chapter.

2

ATTITUDE IS EVERYTHING

Whether becoming a full-time or a part-time real estate investor is the goal, attitude is the most important part of an investment career. In essence, a real estate investor is an entrepreneur and needs to think like one. All entrepreneurs, no matter what their field, achieve success by learning the following attributes. In many ways, this is the most important chapter of the book, so study its contents carefully to ensure that these attributes are already possessed or can be developed.

CLEAR GOALS

Numerous studies have shown that a common characteristic of successful people in all walks of life is the ability to formulate clear goals and then commit to achieving them. Goals provide you clarity and prevent a person from wandering off the path of success. In a later chapter, we will discuss how to set goals in a systematic fashion, but, for now, remember that goals are not something that are simply written down on paper and referred to now and then. They should be something kept in mind every day. And do not think of them in the abstract. Visualize them in very concrete terms. Follow the advice of motivational expert, Denis Waitley:

> *"The secret to productive goal setting is in establishing clearly defined goals, writing them down, and then focusing on them several times a day with words, pictures, and emotions as if we have already achieved them."*

A POSITIVE MENTAL ATTITUDE

A person may or may not be an optimist by nature — many entrepreneurs are. For those who are not natural optimists, do not despair. A positive mental attitude can be developed. It is a simple matter of realizing that optimism is an indispensable asset for achieving success. The clear goals mentioned above will help in maintaining a positive mental attitude because they provide definite targets to aim for and push negatives into the background — or out of the mind entirely.

Another method that can be used to gain and maintain optimism is the use of "affirmations" or "positive assertions." These are simple statements that can be written down on Post-It® Notes and then pasted in strategic places. In effect, the brain can be reprogrammed into positive channels with statements like:

- *"Today, I'm one step closer to obtaining the lease option on the $750,000 property."*

- *"Failures never stop me; they only motivate me."*

- *"I will achieve financial security for me and my family."*

- *"I did a great job on that lease option deal."*

Notice that the affirmations above are general, as well as statements specific to real estate. The most powerful motivations are the ones that are specific to one's own life. For those who have trouble coming up with them at first, go on the Internet and type "affirmations examples" into the search window. This will provide plenty of examples to serve as a basis for other statements. There are many spots to place these reminders. Examples are:

- Bathroom mirror
- Car dashboard
- Dresser mirror
- Home/office desk
- Closet door
- Refrigerator door
- Computer monitor
- Wallet
- Front door
- Briefcase
- Telephone
- Books

Be imaginative and find different places to put the assertions.

Another method of achieving optimism is a simple one — avoid people with bad attitudes. Stay away from whiners and nay-sayers. Such people only live in the past and slow others down or divert them from their course completely. Consciously or unconsciously, their goal is to bring others down to their level, stuck in an endless round of self-recrimination and blame. It is a waste of valuable time.

> *"A strong positive mental attitude will create more miracles than any wonder drug."* — Patricia Neal

PERSONAL STRENGTHS

Part of maintaining a positive mental attitude is the ability to focus on personal strengths. Many people do the opposite and focus on their weaknesses. That is a trap to avoid at all costs. Entrepreneurs know they have strengths and weaknesses, but work to build on those strengths and improve or eliminate the weaknesses. For those who doubt their intelligence, it is time to get rid of that feeling. To succeed in the real estate market all one needs to be is committed and tenacious. Remember Thomas Edison's well known quote:

> *"Genius is one percent inspiration, ninety-nine percent perspiration."*

A person may have personal strengths they are unaware of. A good way to find out is to ask family, friends, business colleagues, etc. for an objective skill assessment. Write down the results on a piece of paper. Use the list to figure out how to build on personal strengths. This can also be done with weaknesses, except they will be reduced or eliminated.

SELF-MOTIVATION

It is important to be a self starter in the real estate field. That means the ability to motivate oneself needs to be developed. Writing down goals is the first step to self-motivation. However, goals on paper mean nothing if the steps to achieve those goals are not carried out. The discipline and motivation to take those steps is needed. Call it "stick-to-it-ness" or any other name, but take action. Avoid procrastination. Do not waste time on any task that is not directly related to the goals. This may mean some sacrifices in the present, but those sacrifices will pay off in a secure financial future.

> "One of the things that my parents have taught me is to never listen to other people's expectations. You should live your own life and live up to your own expectations, and those are the only things I really care about." — Tiger Woods

A DEEP COMMITMENT TO LEARNING

Knowledge of the real estate market is important. Ignorance will always cost money. It is important to gain the necessary knowledge to operate effectively in the area of lease options. Equally important, however, is a commitment to continual and lifelong learning. Local market conditions change, financial instruments change, the national economy changes — change is constant and keeping up with it is necessary to stay on top of the game. Keep this basic rule in mind:

> The more you learn, the more opportunities you will spot, and the greater profitability you will enjoy!

PERSEVERANCE

Sometimes the hardest thing to do in business is to "keep on keeping on." That is, persevering in the face of negativity. Generally speaking, negativity comes from two sources. The easiest source to identify is that of competitors and others in the lease option world (realtors, tenants, etc.). This type of negativity, while not fun, is relatively easy to deal with because the cause can be clearly identified. It is much harder to pinpoint another source of negativity — family and friends. In the case of family, often they are simply scared of the new direction being taken. Security is often very important to them and if they see that security threatened, they may react negatively. The emotional ties with one's family are quite powerful and can undermine resolve. Be determined to persevere and keep in mind the ultimate financial goal.

In the case of friends, they may be jealous of an independent spirit and envy courage. They may unconsciously make statements like, "You are crazy to give up your job," "Most businesses fail within five years," "Nobody really makes money on those types of deals," etc. These are all invitations to give up and fall back into the pack of those who lack a vision of financial freedom. All successful entrepreneurs, whether in real estate or other fields, never give up on their vision. They constantly drive forward. If they meet an obstacle, they find a way around it, over it, under it, or they eliminate the obstacle altogether. They simply do not allow negativity into their lives because they know it is a waste of time. They work on their strengths to build confidence and they take an objective look at their weaknesses, actively seeking to eliminate them and turn them into assets. Later in the book, we will learn how to create strengths and reduce or eliminate areas of weakness to achieve a powerful and confident attitude.

One last note on this subject: One way to eliminate or reduce negativity from family is to keep them informed. That is, do not suddenly announce the decision to go into lease options or some other area of real estate without consulting family members. This is unfair to them and a surefire recipe for negativity. Sit down with them, explain the plan very clearly, the reasons for doing it, and the benefits the family will receive from the course of action. Ask for their support and understanding. Involve them in the process so they feel like a part of the new venture. They may feel uncomfortable with the change at first, but eventually they will get on board and become a part of the team. Finally, remember Benjamin Franklin's words:

> *"Energy and persistence conquer all things."*

COMPLETE COMMITMENT TO SUCCESS

Success in the area of lease options is desired. But true entrepreneurs commit to success in every aspect of their lives — jobs, family, community, etc. They know success in one area breeds success in other areas and they expand their scope beyond their personal lives. They want success for everyone in their lives. Call it "pragmatic altruism." By spreading and sharing success, entrepreneurs better the world and reap the reward for their efforts — increased business and increased community standing.

> *"If you care at all, you will get some results. If you care enough, you'll get incredible results."*
>
> — Jim Rohn, motivational speaker and author

COMMITMENT TO ETHICAL BEHAVIOR

The greatest asset a person has in the real estate market is his or her reputation. Beyond the obvious fact that ethical behavior is the right thing to do, it also has ramifications for one's future in lease options or any other area of the market. People want to deal with individuals they can trust and who will keep their word. In fact, they will want to keep doing business with them over a long period of time. A good reputation is a good investment in one's financial future. On the other hand, a reputation for shady dealing will kill a real estate career quickly. Word spreads fast and the unscrupulous individual soon finds himself or herself shut out of the market. Unethical behavior is morally wrong and stupid from a financial point of view. Committing to ethical practices and being a role model for the industry will provide the satisfaction of doing the right thing. It will allow a person to enjoy a long and profitable career with the respect of everyone.

> *"Always do right — this will gratify some and astonish the rest."*
>
> — Mark Twain, American author and humorist

Now that we have established the characteristics needed to succeed in the real estate market, let us get into the nuts and bolts of lease options.

3

TYPES OF LEASE OPTIONS

As stated earlier, a real estate option provides the right to buy a property without the obligation of having to buy it. The person who sells the option is the *optionor*. The buyer of the option is called the *optionee*.

In order for the optionee to buy the option, he or she normally has to put up a percentage of the agreed-upon purchase price. Because it is negotiable, this percentage varies but is normally within the range of 0.5 to 10 percent. This is known as an *option fee*. For example, if a person is the buyer of an option on a $300,000 property and the option fee percentage is 5 percent, then the option fee is $15,000.

Option Fee Calculation	
Purchase price =	$300,000
Option fee percentage =	x 5%
Option fee =	$15,000

This fee may or may not go toward the purchase price. If the optionee does not exercise the option and buy the property, the optionor keeps the fee. On the other hand, if a person is the buyer and decides to exercise the option, then he or she can apply the option fee against the purchase price as shown on the next page.

Option Fee Applied Against Purchase Price	
Purchase price =	$300,000
Option fee =	$ 15,000
Remaining balance =	$275,000

It may seem odd not to apply the option fee against the purchase price; however, there are situations where it makes sense. For example, a home builder may deal with real estate developers and acquire finished lots from them. Using the option period, the builder agrees to buy the lots within the specified period of time. The developer gets a non-refundable option fee as a percentage of the purchase price. Choosing this course limits the builder's exposure to the amount of the option fee. Due to market fluctuations, personal financial condition, etc., home building can be a risky business and it always pays to reduce risk. This type of option is known as a *purchase option.* It is a way to potentially make big money. This is a strategy more geared to the full-time investor.

The other type of option is the one we will be concentrating on in this book — a standard lease option. This is a strategy suitable for both the part-time and the full-time investor. In this case, the seller options the property to the investor who then may or may not buy the property. If the investor chooses not to buy the property, then he or she may, in turn, sell the option to a buyer. This is known in the trade as a "sandwich" lease. Graphically, it looks like this:

In this case, the object is to be the one in the middle — the investor. That is because a profit can be made on the difference between what is paid for the home and what it can be sold for. Here is a basic example: Assume the lease option is bought from George (the seller) for a stated period (12 months, 18 months, etc.). Under the arrangement, a monthly lease amount of $1,000 must be paid. The investor then turns around and sublets the property to Alice and requires her to pay $1,500 per month. The $500 is the investor's profit (minus expenses, etc.). The lease between the investor and Alice is considered the "sandwich." In later chapters, we will discuss how to make this arrangement even more profitable. In most instances, this is a buying strategy and is a good way to generate income.

There are many other benefits to the standard lease option. First, a significant amount of cash is not required to get into the game. Minimum money or, in some cases, zero down can be offered. Second, the risk is small. Remember, when a property is bought on a lease option, the lease option holder is also reserving the right not to buy it. If the market rises, the holder can buy; if it declines, it is not necessary to buy. Third, the monthly rent paid to the owner is quite a bit less than a mortgage payment. Fourth, there is no qualifying procedure hassle with lenders or mortgage brokers. All that has to be done is build a good personal bond with the seller or a realtor (the subject of a later chapter). Fifth, there can be a good return on the investment. Little or nothing down is being put down and, in return, income and a profit are being received. Finally, in many cases, a seller will be helped out. They may have an unexpected illness, loss of a job, or other issues and the purchase of the option has made a bad situation good for them.

If, for some reason, a standard lease option or a purchase lease cannot be obtained from a seller, try the "subject-to" strategy. Note that this is a buying strategy only. It involves a seller deeding the property while the existing mortgage is still in place. In other words, there is no formal assumption of that mortgage loan. Instead of taking out a new mortgage, the buyer simply starts making the payments. In this case, the lender is not contacted and the buyer purchases the property "subject to" the existing financing. Here is an example: Assume a property is taken over with an actual value of $85,000 for the balance of $70,000. The mortgage on this property has an interest rate of six percent and a monthly payment of $420. It is sold for the actual market value of $85,000 with $8,000 down and then the balance of $77,000 is financed at 10 percent. The buyer's payment will be $675 per month. The result is that $8,000 in cash up front and $250 per month for the next 30 years will be received. Of course, this strategy is pursued by buying several properties and adding the income up. There are other significant benefits by following a subject-to course. Properties can be acquired with a minimum outlay of cash or even, in some cases, no money at all. Also, no financing is required. In addition, ownership of the property is gained with no time consuming process involved. Finally, it can provide a great return on an investment in the long run.

Note, however, that there are definite risks with the subject to strategy. The loans may have "acceleration" or "due on sale" clauses. These clauses allow the lender to call the loan due if the property is transferred. If that happens, it might be necessary to refinance or sell the property. However, most lenders only tend to be concerned with receiving full payments on time. Also, the property is owned and there is a duty to the seller even if market shifts occur or it cannot be sold. In essence, full ownership is obtained, along with all the responsibilities that come with it. Moreover, attention must be paid to the laws of the state. In some, it can be a breach of a contract clause. In that case, a mortgage broker or realtor may be liable for fines or even subject to a revocation of their license.

This chapter has provided basic knowledge about lease options. However, do not be satisfied with basic information. Become further educated on this subject by learning everything possible. Study the local market, consult with others in the business, join business groups, read books and articles, view videos or DVDs, take classes — in other words, work to always learn more. If possible, find mentors who are willing to teach the ins and outs of the business. In return for their invaluable knowledge and experience, give back to them. All in all, learning is an essential part of any investment and a secure financial future!

4
GETTING STARTED

As a budding full- or part-time real estate investor, the first step to take is to set goals to steer a safe, steady, and profitable course. We cannot emphasize how important it is to set goals. As stated in the earlier chapter on attitude, one of the universal characteristics of successful people in every walk of life is that they set clear goals and then do everything they can to reach those goals. Goal setting is one of those traits that elevate achievers above the average person. Research has demonstrated several reasons why goal setting is so powerful and effective:

- *Focus* — Setting goals trains people to focus primarily on important elements of their projects. This prevents the wasting of time on nonproductive activities.

- *Efficiency and effectiveness* — The ability to focus on only important elements enables people to organize their efforts in the most effective and efficient manner possible. This helps lay a straight line toward achievement of goals.

- *Persistence* — Clear goals make people persistent because they then become tangible. In effect, they become real and, therefore, highly achievable.

- *Creativity* — As with any activity, the more experience that can be gained at goal setting, the better one will become at it. New and better strategies will be developed that will, in turn, increase one's ability to increase income with lease options and other forms of real estate strategies. All of this accumulated knowledge and experience will create synergy.

All in all, goal setting is one of the most important tools in a real estate investing kit. As Nido Qubein, a business consultant, said:

> "Goal setting illuminates the road to success just as runway lights illuminate the landing field for an incoming aircraft."

A study of successful people will show that they set goals in everything they do. There is one characteristic in particular in those goals — they are all very specific. Most people make the mistake of setting vague goals like, "I want to be happy" or "I want success." These are not really goals; they are more like unfulfilled longings because there are no specifics on how to achieve them. Everybody wants to be happy and successful; it is those people who get specific who actually become happy and successful. But goals are general in nature and must be converted into specific actions or steps to be achieved.

Now it is time to look at how to set goals. The most effective method is the time-tested and proven SMART system. SMART stands for:

S = Specific

M = Measurable

A = Action Oriented

R = Realistic

T = Time Bound

Let us take a closer look at each of these terms so we can understand exactly what they mean and, at the same time, apply them to the task of acquiring core skills.

Specific — A goal should say what the real dream is in terms that are as specific as possible. A "fuzzy" goal would be, "I want to be a real estate investor." A specific goal would be, "I want to be a full-time investor specializing in lease options, and I need to acquire the skills to accomplish that goal." That last goal very clearly defines what is going to be done with the dream.

Measurable — If a goal, is not measurable, it may be hard to tell when it has been reached. Build milestones into the goals. Again, a fuzzy goal would be, "I want to acquire a lease option soon as a first step in becoming a real estate investor." The word "soon" is too vague. It does not set a specific date and action. A better, more specific goal would be, "I want to acquire my first lease option by Oct. 1, 2007 as a first step toward becoming a full-time real estate investor." This specific goal permits progress toward the dream to be monitored in a very clear and easy manner.

Action Oriented — Once a goal has been set, the steps that will be taken to achieve the goal must be written out in very specific terms. The steps should be action oriented so progress toward the goal can be monitored. Action oriented means each step should be a physical action. For example, let us assume that a person has no experience in real estate or lease options and needs to acquire knowledge on these subjects. A good action step would be, "Call the admissions office at ABC Community College to discuss the real estate offerings by December 1." Making the call is a definite, physical action on a specific date.

Realistic — The goal should be one that is achievable. For example, being a real estate investor on the level of Donald Trump may be a goal, but that is not an immediately realistic goal – although it could be a long-term one. First, the right skills, knowledge, and attitude to get started in the business must be acquired. Set goals that are realistically achievable.

Time Bound — Every goal should have a completion date. This prevents indulging in vagueness and putting action steps off. An example of a timely goal would be: "I want to complete my community college coursework by June 10 of 2007."

The best way to learn how to set goals is to practice, and there is no time like the present. The following pages contain a sample action plan. Use this as a model. Then, use the blank plan on the page following the model by writing down a goal in the blank provided near the top of the page. Complete the form by spelling out the action steps and dates that will need to be taken to accomplish that goal.

Here is a reminder to close this chapter: Do not think of goals only on a long range basis. Remember to also to carry them out on a daily basis. In other words, a long range goal is a strategy. But, in order to achieve that goal, tactics, or short range goals, need to be carried out.

SAMPLE ACTION PLAN

Directions:

Use the blank provided below to write out one of your goals as a lease option investor. Then use the form to list specific action steps to reach that goal and the dates by which you will complete those steps.

Overall goal:

My goal is to: <u>Become a full-time real estate investor specializing in lease options.</u>

Action Step	Completion Date
Contact the admissions office at ABC Community College to discuss the curriculum.	Dec. 1, 2007
Enroll part-time at ABC Community College.	Jan. 10, 2008
Continue	Ongoing
Complete ABC Community College training.	June 10, 2008
Obtain financing to buy my first lease option.	Sept. 1, 2008
Buy first lease option.	Sept. 15, 2008
Sell first lease option and use profits to buy next properties.	Jan. 1, 2009

MY ACTION PLAN

Overall goal:

My goal is to: _____

Action Step	Completion Date

5

SOME BASIC PRINCIPLES

Before committing to action, one must take a good, hard, objective look at his or her financial situation. For those who wish to be full-time investors, it is absolutely essential to have capital on hand to cover any short-term losses due to vacancies between tenants.

YOUR CREDIT RATING

The credit rating is the first place lenders will look. Those with a history of credit problems or bankruptcies will likely pay a steep price for that history. Lenders want the highest possible security for the money they lend; they are not in the business of charity. Lenders will charge those with a shaky credit history higher interest rates than they would for someone with a good or great credit history. More will be paid in loan origination fees (points) and greater down payments will be made. By law in the United States, a person is entitled to one free credit report per year; however, it is recommended to check it every six months just to make sure any errors have not crept into the report. This can be done easily by ordering credit reports from the "big three" in America. The contact information is as follows:

- Equifax Credit Information Services, Inc.
  P.O. Box 740241
  Atlanta, GA 30374-0241
  1-800-685-1111
  www.equifax.com

- Experian
  National Consumers Assistance Center
  P.O. Box 2002
  Allen, TX 75013
  1-888-EXPERIAN (1-888-397-3742)
  www.experian.com

- Trans Union Corp
  Consumer Disclosure Center
  P.O. Box 1000
  Chester, PA 19022
  Toll-free: 1-800-916-8800
  Direct: 610-690-4909
  www.transunion.com

Take these steps when a credit report is received. First, review it carefully. Often, credit files contain out-of-date or incorrect information. This lowers the credit rating. For example, those with common names may get confused and the information may get mixed up. Here are some guidelines for reviewing a credit report:

- Search for anything that is out-of date. This could include items like paid tax liens older than seven years, bankruptcies older than ten years, settled lawsuits, etc.

- Identify misleading or incorrect information such as an incorrect name, address, or social security number; incorrect account histories; duplicate accounts; paid taxes; or liens listed as unpaid, etc.

If problems are found on the credit report, dispute the incorrect information in one of three ways — online, by telephone, or by mail. The easiest and quickest is the online option.

If mail is preferred, write to the addresses listed. In the letter, be sure to ask for a *Request for Investigation* form. Once this form is received, fill it out by listing each error. It is the law that the credit bureau must reply within 30 days on the results of an investigation. Often, they will reply sooner, but if they are late, follow up with another letter.

If the telephone is preferred, call one of the numbers listed. Ask the customer representative for a *Request for Investigation* form because errors have been found on the credit report.

If going online is preferred, use the "status of dispute" service provided by the major credit bureaus. If a credit report has been ordered, a running report of the dispute's status will be given as long as the report number, social security number, name, and ZIP code are provided. The information will be removed if the credit bureau made an error.

The credit bureau will need to be spoken with if there is a disagreement about the incorrect information. Call one of the numbers listed and explain the situation calmly and quietly. Be persistent, but do not yell or get angry. It does not help to seem desperate or out of control. If there is still a disagreement, information can be added to the credit report that will explain the consumer's side of the story. It is the consumer's right to add a short statement of 100 words or less if it is believed that a credit bureau is adding incorrect information to the report. The credit bureau is only required to provide a summary of this statement so the shorter the statement is, the more likely it is that the credit bureau will include it in unedited form.

If the incorrect information cannot be agreed on, it may be necessary to talk directly to the creditors (banks, credit card companies, etc.). First, ask them to remove the incorrect information. Then, demand that they ask the credit bureaus to delete the incorrect items. Write to the customer service department, president, CEO, or someone at the company with the authority to meet the demands.

If, for some reason, the incorrect information was reported by a collection agency, send the agency a copy of the letter as well and ask for a removal of that information. If a creditor is locally-based, visit them personally. Be calm, but firm while explaining the situation. Ask to see a manager, supervisor, CEO, or president. Do not leave until someone agrees to a meeting. Remember: The consumer has a right to a meeting because this creditor has verified incorrect information, and it needs to be removed from the credit report. The general rules of the Fair Credit Reporting Act (FCRA) are provided below. This act specifies rules for how and when creditors report information to credit bureaus. Creditors must follow these regulations:

- Not report information they know is false.

- Not ignore information they know contradicts what they have on file.

- Refrain from reporting incorrect information when they learn that this information is, indeed, incorrect.

- Supply credit bureaus with the correct information when they learn that the information they have been supplying is incorrect.

- Notify credit bureaus when information is disputed.

- Record when accounts are "closed by the consumer."

- Supply credit bureaus with the month and year of the delinquency of all accounts marked for collection, charged off, etc.

- Complete their investigation of the dispute within the 30-45 day period in which the credit bureaus must complete their investigation of the matter.

Take a copy of these rules along for the meeting so they can be referred to. They can be used to remind the creditor of his or her obligations under the law.

Do not forget that positive information can be added to a credit report to improve the rating. This is an essential step to take in raising one's credit score. Remember, positive information may not always be included on a credit report. It is a fact that creditors do not report it to the credit bureaus. If positive information is missing from a credit report, do the following:

- Send a copy of a recent account statement and copies of canceled checks to the credit bureau(s). This demonstrates the payment history.

- Ask the credit bureaus to add the information to the file. The bureaus may charge a small fee for this. They are not required to add information but will normally do so.

Be sure to check the credit report from all three credit bureaus. Some positive information may be on one report, but not on the others. This will save time and ensure that all the reports are consistent.

If a credit rating is not perfect, things can be done to improve it. An important step is to show that one's life is stable. Besides getting paid on time, the one thing creditors love to see in their customers is evidence of stability. Stability is evidence of low risk. That is why teachers, for example, have great credit ratings. As a group, they are highly stable, committed to the community, and are in a public position where risky behavior is less likely.

To show stability, first review the credit reports and see if any of the information listed below is missing. If it is, ask the credit bureaus to add it. Here is information that may need to be added:

- **Present employment:** Employer's name and address and the job title.

- **Previous employment history:** Include this especially if the present job has been held less than two years. Again, include the employer's name and address and the job title.

- **Current residence:** If the residence is owned, be sure to say so. This is good evidence of stability.

- **Previous residence:** Add this especially if the present address has been lived at for less than two years.

- **Telephone number:** Lenders who cannot reach a person by phone are reluctant to grant credit. To them, having no phone or an unlisted number is evidence of instability and, thus, high risk.

- **Date of birth:** Creditors cannot discriminate against a person on the basis of age; on the other hand, they need this information to help verify a person's identity. It also helps prevent confusion for those have very common names like Smith or Jones.

- **Social security number:** Again, this information distinguishes a person from everybody else.

- **Bank checking or savings account number:** This is great evidence of stability as far as lenders are concerned.

Credit bureaus are not required to add this information, but often will because it helps prevent accidental mixing of files. When a request is sent in, be sure to provide documentation that proves the information is true. Include copies of such items as canceled checks, pay stubs, bills, or other proof.

A topic of great concern lately has been credit damage due to identify theft. Identify theft is a growing problem. It is too easy for thieves to steal identities because it is a silent crime. That is, they can get loans in a person's name, open credit card accounts, buy a car, etc., and sneak away with the goods until the victim starts getting notices and calls about purchases they have never made. One reason identify theft is so popular is because it is so easy. Thieves can steal personal information from a person's mailbox, trash, wallet, and on the Internet. Or it can be as simple as a thief looking over someone's shoulder at an ATM and memorizing the PIN number. But the worst part of identify theft may not be the financial damage. The worst part can be the months of hassle in dealing with lenders, credit card companies, other financial institutions, and police departments. Many of these institutions assume that a person is guilty until proven innocent. The best way to avoid identity theft is prevention. Here are some guidelines for prevention:

- If possible, change passwords and PIN numbers often. Do not write them down where thieves can get a hold of that information. Also, do not use obvious items as passwords (birth dates, children's names, etc.).

- Closely review monthly statements for any unauthorized charges.

- Get a copy of a credit report on a yearly basis and review it closely.

- Make sure to keep credit card receipts — do not throw them away in public.

- Shred or tear up those pre-approved credit cards received in the mail.

- Never, ever give personal information out over the telephone unless the person calling is personally known.

- Never, ever give out a social security number to anyone.

- If possible, do not put personal information on a computer home page or other personal profile.

If a person is a victim of identity theft, they need to:

1. File a police report immediately. Make several copies of the report because collection agencies, banks, credit bureaus, etc. may require a copy.

2. Contact every institution to whom money is owed — banks, credit card companies, utility and phone companies, etc. Talk to someone in the fraud department to explain the situation and follow up with a letter as added insurance.

3. Immediately close every account that has been hit by the thief.

4. Ask lenders to place a "fraud" or security alert on accounts that are still good; that is, accounts which have not been the target of the thief.

5. Immediately call the three credit bureaus listed in this chapter and request that they place a fraud alert statement in the file. Also, request that they add a statement asking that creditors call before opening any new account or changing the present accounts.

6. If checks have been stolen, report them to:

   - Telecheck, 1-800-366-501 or **http://www.telecheck.com**
   - National Processing Company, 1-800-255-1157 or **http://www.npc.net/**

7. Contact the post office and find out if the thief may have filed a change of address form.

8. If there are false local phone charges and getting them removed is posing a problem, contact the local public utilities commission for local service providers.

9. If there are false long distance phone charges, contact the Federal Communications Commission (FCC) at **http://www.fcc.gov/** or at 1-888-225-5322 (general information).

10. If a social security number has been stolen and falsely used, call 1-800-269-0271 or go to the following site for further information: **http://www.ssa.gov/oig/hotline/index.htm**.

11. If a driver's license number has been stolen, get a new number. Be prepared to show proof of theft and damage.

12. File a complaint with the Federal Trade Commission by calling the hotline at 1-877-IDTHEFT or go to the following site for further information: **http://www.consumer.gov/idtheft/filing_complaintwftc.html**.

13. Finally, consider identify theft protection from an organization like Fair Isaac. Currently, they charge $4.95 a month or $49.95 yearly for a complete protection package. Their Web site is: **http://www.myfico.com/Products/IDF/Description.aspx?lpid=GGLE2009**.

YOUR CURRENT FINANCIAL CONDITION

It is wise to take an objective look at one's current finances. Despite what many gurus say, lease options are not a "no money down" path to real estate heaven. Particularly for those planning on becoming full-time investors will need income or a cash reserve to fall back on. The rewards of lease options can be great, but there are risks and it is necessary to be prepared for them.

A simple first step to take is to prepare a budget to determine what the income is versus the expenses. If the income is adequate and investing in lease options is desired, cut expenses and save that added cash for investment. If it is hard to do, remember that a future of financial freedom is being created and there will be plenty of time in that future to enjoy the finer things of life. There are always expenses that can be cut; small, daily sacrifices can reap great, future rewards.

A second step is to reduce or eliminate debt, if possible. Pay off that car or furniture loan. Avoid the temptation to pay for goods and services by credit card. If a credit card is a necessity, shop for the ones with the lowest interest rates. Reducing or eliminating debt demonstrates that a person has an essential quality for any real estate transaction: discipline.

A third step to take is to get a financial education, particularly those planning on being a full-time investor. A fundamental knowledge of financial documents such as profit and loss statements, balance sheets, and operating statements is necessary. These will not be needed at the basic level of lease options, but they will be invaluable when moving into more complex areas of real estate. Financial knowledge will enable a person to leverage the initial lease option transactions into greater profitability and a secure future.

ORGANIZE YOUR OFFICE

This is the Digital Age and there is no reason not to enjoy the many benefits of financial and organizational computer applications. With a single property lease option in hand, software for accounting purposes will not be needed. A pad and a pencil will do. However, if multiple lease options are acquired and/or property management is a goal, we recommend getting familiar with the software programs available on the market today. They will come in handy as investments expand and allow more difficult accounting procedures to be handled. Spreadsheet programs like Microsoft Excel or general accounting packages like Quicken or QuickBooks can be used for streamlining all basic accounting requirements. Once beyond that level, however, software designed specifically for property management will be needed. From our companion book, *The Real Estate Investor's Handbook*, here is what to look for in software:

Necessary Requirements in Property Management Software

- A complete accounting package (general ledger, accounts receivable/accounts payable along with check writing, budgeting and financial reporting capabilities. Ability to track work orders and reminders, prints late notices, leases, checks, 1099s, etc.

- Tenant and lease management capabilities (including rental management forms). Pop-up reminders to remind of late rent, expiring leases, etc. categorized by building, unit, owner, or tenant.

- Capabilities to organize tenants, contractors, etc.

- Templates for letters and forms, etc.

A search on the Internet will provide references to many programs. Simply type "property management software" into the window. Below is a partial list of software package names and their URLs in alphabetical order. Choose the program that meets needs and is easiest to understand. Many sites will provide a free trial period.

- MRI Residential — **http://www.realestate.intuit.com/**

- RentRight — **http://www.rent-right.com/**

- Spectra — **http://www.spectraesolutions.com/**

- Tenant File — **http://www.tenantfile.com/**

- TenantPro — **http://www.propertyautomation.com/**

Any of these programs can be customized to fit specific needs. Whichever program is used, review the reports it generates carefully. The information can help spot problems and improve the overall profitability of the property.

Note: At some point in the future when multiple properties have been accumulated, consider having a management company do the accounting. Be sure that reports are received a week or two after the end of each accounting month. Review this information carefully, but do not think of it as a review. What is really being done is learning on a continuous basis — learning how to cut costs, improve profitability, and storing knowledge that will become crucially important as real estate investments grow.

6

GATHERING KNOWLEDGE OF THE REAL ESTATE MARKET

Once a goal has been set as an investor and it has been determined that one's financial condition is in an optimum shape, it is time to study the market to find out where the bargains are. Inexperienced investors will probably want to start in the single-family residential market. It is less complicated than the market for apartment complexes and other housing units. Once experience is gained, consider venturing into multiple-unit dwellings or commercial/industrial properties. See the end of the chapter for investment possibilities in this area.

Here is the golden rule of lease options or any other type of real estate transaction:

Know thy local market!

Or, to put it another way: Those who do not know the market will end up out of business fast. Knowledge of local conditions is everything in real estate. That is because knowledge helps a person make informed buying decisions — and those are the only kind to make. To gain information, we recommend tapping into all of the following sources:

- **Local business/real estate print publications** — These are invaluable sources for information. Read all of them to get a sense of supply and demand, properties available, current trends, etc.

- **Internet sites** — Log on to the local Chamber of Commerce site, business sites, university/college sites, and real estate sites for up-to-date information.

- **Media broadcasts** — Often, there are local television and radio broadcasts specializing in real estate topics. Watch for individuals who are very successful in the business and study their techniques. Learn from the best.

- **Network** — Attend the appropriate functions with local business leaders and real estate professionals. This is an especially important tactic because it puts a person in touch with what is actually happening in the market. Networking is important for two other reasons. One, it helps with the establishment of a "circle of influence;" that is, a group of people who can help a beginner gain a foothold in lease options. Remember this important point:

> Contacts are everything
> in the real estate market.

Two, networking may help a beginner find a mentor who is willing to be a guide through the intricacies of the local market. As stated earlier, this is not a one-way street; be willing to give in return. The quickest way to short-circuit a real estate career is to establish a negative reputation as someone who uses people without consideration for their needs.

Of course, all this knowledge is gathered for one purpose — to find value! Ideally, undervalued properties that can turn a handsome profit are being sought. To achieve that profit, criteria needs to be set for the types of property that are to be controlled with lease options. But to set specific criteria it pays to have an overall picture of the market. First, we will consider general guidelines for market analysis, and then we will outline more specific criteria for lease options.

GENERAL MARKET ANALYSIS GUIDELINES

Here are several broad categories to analyze. These categories apply in any type of real estate transaction, not just lease options.

Category 1: Location

Where an investor buys does matter in a big way, so be sure to study geographic areas carefully before investing in any property. It is usually best to choose a local area for the following reasons:

- It is easier to gain knowledge about it and increase expertise rapidly.

- It is easy to visit and search for properties.

- It keeps costs down, makes the process manageable, and allows a person to become an expert quickly.

Learn everything possible about the local market — property values, rental, rates, school systems, etc. The more knowledge that can be gained, the easier it will be to evaluate lease option possibilities and make sound decisions.

Finding good locations is a process of elimination. Look for growing areas with a strong economic engine. Check out neighborhoods that are in the path of progress; there is more information on this subject in Category 7. They should have great quality retail shops, recreational centers, be easily accessible to work, and have schools with excellent reputations. Look for neighborhoods in transition from not-so-hot status to gentrification status. People find these areas highly desirable and the buzz can move residential and business property prices up for you.

Category 2: Type

Property type is the second essential criterion. Know what is being looked for — single family home, multi-unit dwellings, etc. Each type has its advantages.

- **Single Family** — These properties appreciate well over time and there is always a demand for them. Also, emotion can drive prices up since buying a home is such a personal decision.

- **Multi Family** — These investments generate cash flow. In addition, rents tend to go up over time. These two markets tend to operate in an inverse way; that is, when housing is affordable, rents go down and vacancies go up. When housing is expensive, then rents go up.

- **Commercial/industrial** — These properties offer bigger potential growth and appreciation, but also a much bigger risk. Unemployment, slow economic conditions, overbuilding, etc. can affect the returns on this type of investment.

Category 3: Property Worth

It is important to know what properties are worth within a chosen geographic area so study them closely. Profitability depends on it. First, decide what price range can be operated in. Then, figure out the discount that will be required in order to purchase the lease option. Once these criteria are established, learn property values and rents. This information can be found by doing the following:

- Talk to brokers or agents.

- Browse newspaper and Internet listings.

- Physically visit the targeted area. Check out open houses and look at rentals.

- Look for "For Rent" signs and call the numbers on them.

The more properties in the target area are researched and inspected the better the understanding of value will be. As part of the research, ask questions like:

- Are there favorable rental laws?

- Does this neighborhood have a great school that will attract families?

- What is the crime rate?

- Do work, retail, and recreational centers make the property more marketable?

Category 4: Population

Demand for real estate and population are closely related. Simply put, if an area has a steady growth in people, a need for more residential and commercial retail properties will grow and so will the opportunities for the investor. A region cannot be looked at as a whole, however, and not every part of that region will have an increase in population. Look closer and examine local communities and neighborhoods to see which way the demographics are headed. It is wise to proceed as all successful real estate investors do and examine net population growth in submarkets to see where there are positive trends for investment.

Category 5: Job Growth and Levels of Income

Good job growth is vital in any area targeted for investment. It is another simple equation: Good jobs attract people; people need housing; the real estate market grows. A basic source for information on job growth is the U.S. Bureau of Labor Statistics (**http://www.bls.gov/**). This government agency not only tracks job statistics on a national level but also on a state and local level. But this is only a starting point for research. Break down the statistics and get at the reality of the local situation. For example, there may be a job growth in the area, but are they good-paying jobs or do they mostly pay only minimum wage? This is an important fact to know since minimum wage workers are not likely to be in the home-buying market soon.

Also, does the area have a diverse number of companies and jobs? The more diverse the economy is, the less chance an economic downturn will damage or devastate the real estate market. Detroit and Seattle are two examples of the dangers of local economies being tied too tightly to only one or a few manufacturers. As goes the auto and airplane markets, so go Detroit and Seattle. This leads to a boom and bust market and the accompanying uncertainty. Always seek diversity.

Another consideration is the types of industries within the targeted investment area and their prospects for growth. Historically speaking, the farming sector is slow growing, along with small retail and similar sectors, so real estate values will grow slowly as well. On the other hand, if an area with high growth industries such as technology companies is targeted, then real estate values will grow at a faster pace and provide a much better shot at price appreciation. Also, be sure to know what types of jobs are available. For example, if an investor is considering lease options on retail office space and the area has mostly minimum wage jobs, then this is a serious mismatch. Minimum wage workers are not going to rent the space. Instead, an area with professionals who would be interested in the property will be needed. Make sure that the amenities are available for professional people so they will find the area very attractive. The area should have easily accessible restaurants, shops, entertainment venues, etc.

In this era of job outsourcing, check to make sure jobs are not going to move overseas. Without jobs, the investment will stagnate or actually lose value. Look for companies paying stable or increasing wages. That means there is a market for their goods or services and they do not plan on moving production out of the country any time soon. At the same time, check levels of unemployment. Have they been rising or declining? Finally, look for areas that include employment resistant to market downturns (education, government, medical services, etc.).

The Local Area

After checking out the demographic information listed above, zero in on local areas to make sure all the factors for success are in place to ensure success. In general, aim for the middle in terms of the properties being looked at. That is where the greatest success will be found. Avoid declining local areas, overbuilt areas, or areas where demand is weak or non-existent. At the same time, avoid locales where properties are expensive or overpriced. In these spots, damage can be done to an investor's cash flow if he invests; plus, there is little opportunity for appreciation that would make the investment worthwhile. Expensive properties can also be difficult to sell. Look for properties between the two extremes. They are easier to buy, easier to sell, and demand is greater overall. Greater cash flow and appreciation will be enjoyed.

The basic laws of supply and demand apply in the local area just as they do on the regional or national levels. The aim: strong demand and limited supply. This situation creates shortages and opportunities for an investor.

Supply and demand can be evaluated through a number of indicators. For example, the following factors indicate that supply is greater than demand:

- Large number of building permits

- Weak absorption/rental of new properties

- Excess of income property listings

The result is low occupancy, low rents, and rental concessions. This situation ends up costing the investor in terms of lower cash flow and smaller appreciation potential. The following are good indicators that it is time to invest:

- Few vacancies

- Strong absorption/rental of new properties

- Few income property listings

Let us get specific in terms of the indicators that should be looked at to evaluate the "investment worthiness" of a local area.

Building Permits

This is a good place to look at first to determine the investment potential of a particular area or neighborhood. Building permits are a clear indicator about the future real estate supply. If there are too many over a long period of time, it may indicate that future appreciation will not be great because the market will have an oversupply of properties. On the hand, if permits are few, it may indicate that interest rates are too high, the market is saturated, or that other negative factors are influencing the issuance of building permits. In either case, these influences have to be sorted through to make sure that there is a good environment for investment. *Positive absorption* is a situation in which the demand for space is greater than the supply and it is a good measure of how healthy the real estate market is. If available new properties are rented within months, then there is a healthy market. It means the rate at which properties are being rented and occupied is robust. Absorption is measured differently in the residential and commercial markets. Residential properties are measured in housing units while commercial properties are measured in square footage. Avoid negative absorption markets in which real estate properties are being built at a rate greater than the demand for them.

Local planning or building departments can supply information on building permits. Absorption numbers are harder to come by, but they can be obtained from local real estate appraisers and brokers, especially brokers holding Certified Commercial Investment Member (CCIM) certification. They specialize in the sale of income properties and normally track absorption statistics.

Keep in mind that both building permits and absorption are specific to different types of properties. This means one type of property will not have an influence on other types unless the use of a property is changed.

Cost of Renting vs. Cost of Buying

Supply and demand is also affected by the factors of renting versus buying. For example, if there is a situation in which the cost of buying a home is low compared to the cost of renting, renters will buy homes. This increases home sales and lowers demand for rentals. Property listings will often reflect this trend when they increase in number. Such increases can indicate the market is becoming saturated with listings and it is time for investors to move elsewhere. This is because too many listings give buyers the opportunity to be more picky. The result is that prices trend downward, making investment opportunities much less attractive for investors. Avoid this situation by looking for a decrease in property listings. This indicates demand is greater than supply, renters stay put, and the sales relative to listings drop. Prices will trend upward and so will the opportunity for appreciation.

Levels of Occupancy

Another method of measuring supply and demand is the market occupancy rate. The market occupancy rate is defined as the percentage of that type of property available for occupancy that is currently rented. If there is an area with 3,000 total rental units in apartment buildings and there is a 95 percent occupancy rate, then 2,850 are occupied. This means that five percent, or 150, of the units are vacant. If commercial, industrial, or retail spaces are dealt with, occupancy levels will be measured differently, in terms of square footage rather than units.

Market occupancy rate is important because it tells the potential of a particular property. Look for low vacancy rates and a lower number of building permits. This generally shows that real estate prices will appreciate. When low vacancy rates occur, it is a landlord's market. The low rates create higher demand for existing units which, in turn, keeps market prices higher. Avoid high vacancy rates which indicate an oversupply of real estate. This pressures rental rates downward because there is so much competition among landlords for tenants. Look at concessions to see if they signal a weakness in the rental market. Concessions are items like free rent, upgrades, special deals, etc. designed to attract renters. If there are too many concessions being offered, then the rental market may indeed be weak. However, be aware that in some areas concessions are offered as a matter of course and may not be an indicator of market strength or weakness.

Where can information about occupancy rates be found? It can be as simple as doing a walk-through of a commercial, industrial, or retail property. Or, in cases where the rates are obvious trade organizations and industry service providers like the National Apartment Association (**http://www. naahq.org/**) or the Building Owners and Managers Association (**http:// www.boma.org/**) can be consulted. These organizations have local affiliates who can provide the information needed to make informed decisions.

Rental Rates

Rental rates, or rent levels, also provide good indicators of the supply and demand situation for income properties. When real estate demand keeps up with the supply of housing and the local economy is growing, rents generally increase, meaning that real estate prices will continue to appreciate.

Be aware that this information is not always easy to get. Owners and property managers are not keen about letting out this information in soft markets. This is because they do not like present tenants, who were signed at a higher rate, learning that new tenants are getting a lower rent. This can cause trouble managers and owners do not really want. But an investor will be competing against these individuals so he or she needs to find and calculate the effective rental rate. If a rental property is available for $1,500 a month, but the owner is offering a concession of one month's free rent on a yearly lease, then the effective rent is really $1,375 per month. When rates are compared, be sure to include concessions so the rates will be set at competitive levels.

Category 7: The Path of Progress

Ideally, find property that is in the "path of progress." This is simply an area in which a community is going to expand. As the area improves, property appreciates. If the lease-option holder decides to exercise the option and keep the property, he or she also gains other benefits:

- Good tenants are easier to find — and keep.

- Occupancy is higher.

- Turnover is lower.

- Appreciation rates are higher.

In most major cities, there is new construction and growth going on all the time. And certain areas gain prestige; they become areas people really want to live in. Through word-of-mouth, advertising, and other means, they become the place to be. This creates demand and prices and appreciation increase. To find where the path of progress is headed consult the guidelines from our companion book, *The Real Estate Investor's Handbook*:

Path of Progress Guidelines

- **Guideline 1:** Look for major retailers. Companies like Best Buy, Lowes, Costco, and Home Depot do not just build their stores on any old spot. They do an exhaustive amount of research before they select a site, so this means they see potential in the area.

- **Guideline 2:** Check to see where new highways are headed. That shows where properties will likely be available for development.

- **Guideline 3:** Look for cities or neighborhoods where revitalization efforts are taking place. Many times cities with blighted areas form redevelopment districts and offer incentives in order to attract investors. This can be a great opportunity. However, be sure that the local leaders and agencies actually have a clear and definite plan for redevelopment, the revenues to back up that plan, and the political clout to carry through the plan.

Other large investors are on the lookout for the path of progress so it pays to get in early and look for properties that may be overlooked by people or companies with much deeper pockets. In particular, look for single family homes that have the potential for rezoning for commercial use as a professional office building. Be sure to check that similar rezoning requests have been granted. This indicates a favorable climate. A professional office building brings in a much higher rental rate than a single-family dwelling and results in a much higher resale value.

SPECIFIC MARKET ANALYSIS GUIDELINES

Once general market conditions are understood, ask the following questions to establish the criteria for buying lease options:

- What types of properties is the investor interested in buying? (Single family homes, multiunit dwellings, commercial, etc.)

- What price range is best for his or her current situation?

- What percentage of the purchase price can he or she afford to pay for the lease option?

- What are the prime geographic areas for the investments?

The answer to the last question is of vital importance for obvious reasons. Do not buy any kind of property in a neighborhood or commercial area that is going downhill fast, has a high crime rate, etc. This means the market needs to be carefully analyzed both in broad and specific terms before the process of investing in lease options is started. There are plenty of possibilities out there. Here are a few examples to get started on thinking about those possibilities in the area:

Single Family Homes

This is a great area in which to get started in the lease option field since it has lower cost and less risk than in multiunit, commercial, or industrial deals. However, as with any area of real estate, there are negatives which the investor needs to be aware of in order to prevent or overcome them so let us discuss them first. With a sandwich lease in which the property has been subleased to a tenant/buyer, the following things can happen:

- The person may have to be evicted due to a failure to make lease payments.

- A court rules that the person cannot be evicted from the property because he or she has an equitable interest in the property. This means foreclosure proceedings instead of eviction. Foreclosure is a time consuming process which can cost money.

- The person vandalizes or destroys the leased property.

- The property owner refuses to sell after the tenant/buyer has exercised their option. Or the property owner refuses to sell the property at the agreed upon purchase price after the tenant/buyer has exercised their option.

- The tenant/buyer must be relocated after the lease-optioned property is damaged or destroyed by a fire or natural forces.

A more common risk is the simple fact that some investors have not done their research and acquired the knowledge to operate effectively as a residential landlord. Avoid getting hurt financially in the residential lease option market by acquiring basic property management knowledge. Another risk, related to lack of knowledge, is the failure to factor in the amount of time required to manage properties. Many optionees think that if they are receiving a $150 positive cash flow on a property, then that amount is free and clear profit. But, once they analyze the situation closely and total up the amount of time spent on that property as a business expense, reality sets in; they are actually working for an amount far less than projected. Other unexpected costs can occur as well. For example, if a tenant has to be evicted for nonpayment, then the investor has to pay the lease payments until another tenant/buyer is found — and it costs money to find that new buyer. These are all out-of-pocket costs that will have to be met and this can lead to trouble if the cash reserves are not on hand.

Another consideration is the remote possibility that the standard lease option agreement may violate the loan's due-on-sale clause if the lender discovers the lease option agreement. This clause is spelled out in the following federal code.

Code of Federal Regulations
Title 12, Banks and Banking
PART 591 – PREEMPTION OF STATE DUE-ON-SALE LAWS
Section 591.2 (b)

Due-on-sale clause means a contract provision which authorizes the lender, at his or her option, to declare immediately due and payable sums secured by the lender's security instrument upon a sale of transfer of all or any part of the real property securing the loan without the lender's prior written consent. For purposes of this definition, a sale or transfer means the conveyance of real property of any right, title, or interest therein, whether legal or equitable, whether voluntary or involuntary, by outright sale, deed, installment sale contract, land contract, contract for deed, leasehold interest with a term greater than three years, lease-option contract or any other method of conveyance of real property interests.

Most lenders are more concerned with receiving their money than in invoking the due-on-sale clause, but be aware of the possibility that this may occur.

Ethical investors use the lease option strategy honestly and treat both tenant/buyers and lenders with respect. However, scammers have used equity skimming schemes to give the strategy a bad name. Typically, these schemes involve the property owner using the lease option as his or her personal piggy bank. This unethical owner collects an option fee and security deposit at the front end and then collects lease payments over a period of time without making one loan payment to the lender. Once the lending institution discovers this, it forecloses on the loan and evicts the innocent lessee or tenant/buyer, who had no idea the scam was going on. Anyone who engaged in equity skimming is defined under the following U.S. Code. The penalties can be quite stiff for this offense.

Sec. 1709-2. – Equity skimming; penalty; persons liable; one dwelling exemption

Whoever, with intent to defraud, willfully engages in a pattern or practice of –

(1) Purchasing one- to four-family dwellings (including condominiums and cooperatives) which are subject to a loan in default at time of purchase or in default within one year subsequent to the purchase and the loan is secured by a mortgage or deed of trust insured or held by the Secretary of Housing and Urban Development or guaranteed by the Department of Veterans Affairs, or the loan is made by the Department of Veterans Affairs,

(2) Failing to make payments under the mortgage or deed of trust as the payments become due, regardless of whether the purchaser is obligated on the loan, and

(3) Applying or authorizing the application of rents from such dwellings for his own use, shall be fined not more than $250,000 or imprisoned not more than five years, or both. This section shall apply to a purchaser of such a dwelling, or a beneficial owner under any business organization or trust purchasing such dwelling, or to an officer, director, or agent of any such purchaser. Nothing in this section shall apply to the purchaser of only one such dwelling.

Here is a final negative on the standard sandwich lease option. According to Thomas J. Lucier in his book, *How to Make Money with Real Estate Options*, this type of lease option is really an installment sale. He states that, under the terms in a standard agreement, the relationship between the parties is really that of debtor and creditor, not that of lessee-optionee and lessor-optionor. According to Lucier:

> "This debtor-creditor relationship is created whenever the terms of a lease option call for the property owner (lessor-optionor) to credit the option consideration and a fixed portion of the monthly lease payment toward the purchase price when the real estate option is exercised. Once this debtor-creditor relationship is created, the tenant (lessee-optionee) has an equitable or ownership interest instead of leasehold interest in the property lease optioned. When a lease option agreement gives the lessee-optionee an equitable interested in the property being lease optioned, it becomes an installment sales agreement and not a lease option agreement."

In practical terms, what this means is that if a tenant has to be evicted, the owner may have to foreclose instead of evicting the tenant and that is much more costly and time consuming.

Since the sandwich lease option strategy has its limitations, Lucier advocates buying a low cost real estate option on an undervalued single family home which can be leased at a below market rental rate. This saves money on housing costs, but also provides value appreciation while avoiding the costs and financial liabilities of out-and-out ownership. As Lucier points out, most of the benefits of home ownership (no tax advantages) are received without having to qualify for a loan, put down a down payment, pay closing costs, pay for repairs, or buy any property. The key to this strategy is to have two separate transactions: a straight real estate option transaction and a genuine lease transaction. In the lease, the parties' relationship is that of lessee (tenant) and lessor (landlord) and the lessee has a leasehold interest in the leased property. Also, the lessee agrees to pay a monthly lease payment and the lessor agrees to maintain the property during the lease period. According to Lucier, the advantage of this arrangement is that the option agreement will not be automatically voided if the terms of the lease agreement are defaulted on and eviction results. It will still be valid until it is exercised or expires. Lucier also recommends that both the lease and real estate option agreements include assignment clauses. These clauses will allow agreements to be sold to a third party without the property owner's permission. Lucier recommends that a separate memorandum of real estate agreement and a memorandum of lease agreement are recorded as shown in the sample below.

Memorandum of Lease Agreement — Sample

On the 15th day of April, 2007, this memorandum of lease agreement is made for the purpose of recording and giving notice of a lease agreement made between Samuel T. Smith, known hereafter as the Lessor, and John B. Jones, known hereafter as the Lessee, in which the Lessor agrees to lease to Lessee that certain real property known as (address, city, state, ZIP) and legally described as: Lots 2, 3, and 4 of XYZ subdivision according to the map or plat thereof as recorded in plat book 82, page 91 of the public on the 15th day of April, 2007 and which will expire at 12 midnight on the 14th day of April, 2008.

AS WITNESSED, Lessor and Lessee have set their hands to the dates stated above.

Samuel T. Smith   John B. Jones

Lessor   Lessee

In this process, the lessee (tenant) agrees to lease the property from the owner (lessee). The lessee then buys the real estate option from the lessor to purchase the leased property. The option grants the optionee (lessee) the exclusive, unrestricted, and irrevocable right and option to buy the leased property at a fixed purchase price during the option period. The optionee can then assign or exercise the real estate option or let it expire. Once it is exercised, the option agreement converts into a bilateral purchase agreement. In this agreement, the optionee becomes the buyer and the optioner the seller. When the transaction is closed, the seller transfers the property title to the buyer. Lucier recommends that the following stipulations be included in the agreements:

- Two year lease agreement

- Two year real estate option agreement

- A fixed purchase price that is at least 20 percent below the current market value of the property

- A rental rate that is at least ten percent below the fair market rental rate of the property

- A one year extension clause in the lease agreement

- A one year extension clause in the option agreement

Of course, make sure a renter's insurance policy is bought to provide coverage against fire and theft of personal property and personal liability coverage for injuries and damages caused by tenant neglect. Do an Internet search to find renters' insurance coverage or go to these sites:

- Geico — **http://www.geico.com/**

- NetQuote — **http://www.netquote.com/**

- 2Insure4Less — **www.2insure4less.com/**

- WellsFargo — **https://www.wellsfargo.com/**

Lucier also recommends that all lease payments be paid to a licensed loan servicing company to avoid becoming a victim in an equity skimming con as described earlier. This arrangement means the company takes the money they receive as lease payments and uses it pay the lender directly. It also means that there is verifiable proof that the loan payments are being made and are not funding the property owner's scam. Again, search for "licensed loan servicing companies" or visit these sites mentioned by Lucier:

- Note Servicing Center, Inc. — **http://sellerloans.com/**

- PLM Lender Services, Inc. — **http://www.plmweb.com/**

As to the type of property to use the lease and option strategy with, look for homes located in stable neighborhoods with middle income owners. They should have two or three bedrooms, two bathrooms, and an attached garage with a fenced in backyard. Also, look for locations near good schools, parks and playgrounds, offices and industrial parks, shopping malls, medical facilities, etc. To find these properties, contact the owners of vacant houses, relocating owners, military transfers, and out-of-town absentee owners.

"Correctable" Properties

With these types of properties, correctable issues can include problems with cash flow, finances, maintenance, management, ownership, structure, tenants, titles, vacancies, etc. The key issue is that they are correctable at a minimal cost.

Code Violation Properties

Vacant properties are often the target of vandals. Their destructive activities generate calls to the police department from irate neighbors which issues citations for code violations. Generally speaking, these violations must be fixed within 30 to 60 days. If they are not fixed, the owner faces daily fines until the repairs are completed. At worst, if the owner does nothing, the building is condemned. If they are structurally sound, these properties can be a great investment. Single family homes or commercial properties that can be turned around quickly for the cost of cleaning them up are desired.

Mismanaged Rental Properties

Each investor will have to apply his or her own criteria, but look for small rental properties that can be upgraded easily. In cases like this, there may be several reasons why the property is mismanaged. The owner may have neglected the property or hired an incompetent manager who has let upkeep and tenancy slide. Or the owner himself may simply be an amateur who has failed to study the local rental market and rented the property at below-market rates and ended up with a cash flow problem. A poorly managed rental property can be spotted easily enough — building and grounds are neglected, turnover/vacancy rates are high, damage has been done to rental units, rental payments have gone uncollected, etc. A situation like this can be easily turned around through the application of professional property management practices. Check the property ahead of time to make sure there are no structural deficiencies or serious maintenance problems. Also, make sure the property is located in a moderate income neighborhood that is stable and has a low crime rate. It should have easy access to shopping centers, employers, schools, etc. In addition, rents that can be increased by a reasonable amount once the property has been turned around are desired. An investor wants to be able to buy the lease option on a rental property that can be bought for below market value. Be aware that, with this strategy, the area of landlording is being entered.

Obsolescent Properties

This category includes vacant commercial and industrial properties. Their original purpose is gone due to technological or market changes. However, many of them are structurally sound and can be converted to modern and profitable use. An example is a factory building originally used to manufacture agricultural equipment converted to office space. Obsolescent buildings can be particularly attractive as lease option opportunities for several reasons. First, they can be significantly undervalued because no one realizes their potential for modernization. Second, all the complications involved in building new buildings are avoided — a sometimes excruciating building approval process, delays in delivery of building materials, weather delays, cost overruns, lack of qualified workers, etc. Third, they can often be bought at prices well below their replacement cost. Fourth, owners of obsolescent properties are often eager to get the property off their hands and are, therefore, more willing to consider a low cost lease option solution to their problem. Fifth, these properties are generally under the radar of corporate and institutional real estate investors. Sixth, conventional real estate investors most likely will have rejected an obsolescent property as an investment because of the potential risk factor. And, seventh the opportunity to gain quick resale profits is available.

Properties become obsolete for three reasons: One is *functional obsolescence*. This simply means that a property has lost value for one of several reasons. Some buildings outlive their original function. For example, a large Midwestern building devoted to the manufacture of agricultural tractors lost its function when the company was swallowed up by a larger corporation which then decommissioned the plant. Although the building was a solid brick structure, it did not have an appealing design — until a shrewd investor modernized the exterior and converted it into appealing office space. Other factors causing obsolescence can be changing technology, bad economic times, lack of modern amenities, etc.

Another reason is *economic obsolescence*; that is, perhaps the neighborhood has changed and a sewage treatment plant or juvenile offender facility has been constructed on adjoining land. These facilities are perceived as undesirable and cause movement away from the area. Or a new highway may have been constructed, diverting traffic away from the property. These factors can be taken advantage of, for example, by converting such a property into a storage facility for manufacturers unconcerned about facilities like offender facilities and treatment plants.

Finally, there is *physical obsolescence*. This is often due to neglect or mismanagement. As a result, the property loses value. In any of the above cases, target a property that requires minor repairs, modifications, or cosmetic changes. The objective is to turn a profit, not get involved in expensive repairs that eat into that profit.

Be aware that there are four classifications of commercial buildings in the real estate industry. The building classification may rate how the building is generally accepted in the market, or it may be a personal classification by the individual referring to that structure.

- *Class A Building* — This classification refers to the highest quality buildings. They are often newer, large building that have up-to-date amenities such as telecommunication/Internet capabilities and are often located in desirable areas.

- *Class B Building* — This classification describes an average building, one that may be over ten years old with many amenities and located in a desirable area.

- *Class C Building* — A term commonly used to describe a below average building. It may be an older, well-maintained building but have smaller size units. Class C buildings are typically located in stable areas.

- *Class D Building* — These are older buildings which have high vacancy rates, lack of maintenance, few amenities, and are often located in or near marginal areas.

A good strategy is to buy options on properties in Classes C and D that are in the path of progress or areas that are being gentrified. Target owners who do not have the means to convert their obsolescent property to more profitable use.

The key to making the most of lease options on obsolescent properties is imagination. A variety of uses for these properties will need to be visualized because they need to be marketed and made attractive to potential customers. Obsolescents can be promoted as conversions, retrofits, reutilizations, repositions, or any other of the current real estate buzzwords, but be sure to paint a picture in a customer's mind as to the possible uses. For example, a closed and boarded up convenience store may make an excellent conversion to a health foods business. Or a closed party and gift store may offer a good site for a cellular phone business. But go beyond the basic concepts as described in the examples just cited. Do the homework first and find out if such businesses are a good fit for the area. For instance, a health foods business would make good sense if the property is located in a burgeoning area with upwardly mobile, health conscious professionals. That means there is the potential for a large market for the foods and that is extremely attractive to buyers of lease options. That is a benefit that should be highlighted in the property sheets sent out. Be sure to have supporting documentation so the number crunchers have proof of these claims. Once the proof is provided, there is the potential to make a quick profit since opportunities like that are likely to be grabbed up fast depending on the state of the economy.

Once an obsolescent property is identified, the first step is to do a visual inspection from the outside to see if it is a viable opportunity. We recommend making a checklist similar to the one below so that important items that can affect the viability of getting a lease option on the property will not be forgotten.

Sample Checklist for Obsolescent Properties		
1. Electric meter removed from property?	__Yes	___No
2. Electrical power line connected to property?	__Yes	___No
3. Any citations for code violations?	__Yes	___No
4. Water meter removed?	__Yes	___No
5. Any condemnation notices?	__Yes	___No
6. Signs of termite/rodent infestations?	__Yes	___No
7. Signs of mold?	__Yes	___No
8. Any environmental waste on property?	__Yes	___No
9. Other:_____		

The purpose of the checklist is not only to discover obvious problems or lack of them, but also to find out how long the property has been vacant. The longer it has been vacant, the greater the chance a low cost option fee and a below market purchase price can be bargained for.

Use common sense when inspecting an obsolescent property. If there are "No Trespassing" signs posted on the property or on the outside of the building, do not enter. In the first place, it is illegal; in the second, it can be dangerous. In urban areas, there is the possibility that a person could be mistaken for a burglar or that the building might be occupied by people like drug dealers and felons. Needless to say, such circumstances are not healthy for any real estate career!

A final word on obsolescent and any other lease option opportunities: Investors should begin in the local market and learn to know it well. However, once experience has been gained, there is no reason the Internet cannot be used to cast the lease option net wider — particularly in the case of commercial/industrial properties — if possibilities for a particular property have been run out of.

Simply search the Internet to find businesses state wide who might be interested in that property. The key is to identify potential lease option buyers who are searching for a particular facility that meets their needs. For example, if a storage facility is under option, search for companies associated with the storage business. Then, e-mail everyone on the list a property fact sheet along with photographs of the exterior and interior of the building.

Rezonable Properties

There are many definitions of rezoning, including this one:

> *"Rezoning is an act of the local legislature that changes the principal uses permitted on one or more parcels of land or throughout one or more zoning districts. Rezoning includes the amendment of the zoning map, as well as the use provisions in the district regulations applicable to the land that is rezoned."*
>
> **http://www.nymir.org/zoning/glossary.html**

Essentially, rezoning is when a building is converted from one use to another, more profitable use. For example, a vacant building may be bought that is in the path of progress and it may be converted to a coffee shop because many middle class people will be moving into the area to take jobs in the offices of major corporations. Having done the research, it is known that there will be lots of foot traffic due to the vacant building's central location. This makes rezoning a profitable path to take. A bonus for getting an option on a property in the path of progress is that it is less likely that opponents of rezoning will be encountered. Neighbors and the city may welcome and encourage rezoning as a way of improving the area.

The rezoning process involves dealing with the local governmental authorities (town councils, county commissioners, aldermen, etc.), and the process will vary from city to city. However, there are basic steps in any rezoning procedure:

Step 1: Complete a rezoning application.

Step 2: Meet with the appropriate planning/zoning agencies to have them review the application. The application should include a notarized signature of the property owner on an affidavit authorizing agent form. An application fee is normally paid at this time.

Step 3: Mail a written notification of the rezoning request to all the neighboring property owners.

Step 4: Present the rezoning plan to the appropriate planning/zoning authority.

Step 5: The authority makes a recommendation to the local planning/zoning board.

Step 6: Public hearings are held in which comments can be made by the public. The planning board members make recommendations on the request.

Step 7: A final public hearing is held before elected officials. They take a vote to either accept or reject the request.

An example of a 13- step rezoning process is provided at the end of the chapter for your review.

Using the lease option strategy, a property can be controlled during the rezoning process. Then, when the application is approved, the option can either be exercised to buy the property or the option can be resold. A potential negative with rezoning is that the city or county bureaucracy or both may have to be dealt with. It has often been said that bureaucracies exist to protect themselves, so it is essential that staff members are treated with respect and the procedures are followed even though they may be tedious and time consuming. The best path is to consult with officials in a friendly and patient matter. If this is not done, they may end up issuing a "no" recommendation and it is almost a dead certainty that elected officials will follow that recommendation. It also pays to do research and find out which way the wind blows in terms of local politics. If the climate is pro-rezoning, then the request will have easier sailing. If it is not, then some rough seas will have to be navigated in order to reach the rezoning destination. Times for the rezoning process vary. It may take from one month to four months before an application is approved or disapproved.

What should be included in a rezoning application? Again, it varies with the location. Here is an excerpted example from St. Croix County, Wisconsin:

Site Information Applicant Information Request

10 Copies of application packet to include:

- Aerial Photo (can be obtained from county Web site at **www.co.saint-croix.wi.us**)

- Scaled map with **exact** boundaries of parcel to be rezoned

- Drawing: to include short-term or long-term plans for the property indentifying future use, density, layout, etc.

- Completed rezoning questionnaire

- Intersection Warrants Analysis if required*

- Property's most recent tax bill (this can be obtained at the County Treasurer's Office) for proof of ownership

- List of all adjoining land owners' names and mailing addresses (including properties across roadways)

- Metes and Bounds description or boundary description (typically prepared by a registered land surveyor)

$1,000 application fee (non-refundable) payable to St. Croix County Planning & Zoning Department

* You may be required to conduct an "Intersection Warrants Analysis" study to determine the traffic impact and address safety concerns on major roadways. This study is conducted and financed by you and reviewed by the Planning & Zoning Department and St. Croix County Highway Department.

Please Note: Application materials should not include covers, binders, or envelopes. Application packets should be collated and either stapled or paper clipped in the upper left hand corner. All maps, plans and engineering data must be submitted on paper no larger than 11" x 17." The following process takes anywhere from 60 to 90 days to complete.

The rezoning process is a complicated one and needs considerable knowledge to be completed successfully. There are two choices in this matter. An investor can acquire the knowledge and handle the process, or an attorney can be hired who specializes in the areas of land use and zoning. An attorney is the general recommendation. He or she will be able to cut through bureaucratic blather much more quickly, thus making the attorney's fee a cheaper option than going toe-to-toe in an extended fight with experienced governmental in fighters. This strategy also keeps the investor out of the line of fire and helps maintain good relations with the local government.

Before any of the above process commences, the homework needs to be done to find out if the property being looked at can be rezoned and has, in actuality, good profit potential. One way to do this is work with zoning officials in the local area. They may have individuals in positions dedicated to helping with the rezoning process. In combination with this, do research and dig deep to make sure rezoning is feasible and potentially profitable. This usually means:

- Verification of the property's zoning designation.

- Review of previous rezoning applications, government moratoriums, and land use studies.

- Verification of the surrounding properties in terms of zoning designations, rezoning applications, special zoning exceptions, and variances, etc.

- Asking for advice on rezoning from planning and zoning agencies.

When an option is bought on a property that can be rezoned, obtain the optionor's written approval to rezone. This permits the investor to represent him or her before the appropriate zoning agencies. The title of the document varies with state and location, but may be called an "agent's affidavit" or "affidavit to authorize agent." It gives a person the right to sign any documents necessary for the filing of a rezoning application. Be sure this document is signed at the same time the option agreement and title transfer documents are signed and notarized. Also, make sure the option period extends beyond the time it takes for an application to be approved. Generally speaking, an option in the eight to twelve month period should protect the investment.

7

UNDERSTANDING REAL ESTATE MARKET PSYCHOLOGY AND VALUE

———

One day the stock market rises, only to fall the next. But what drives this movement? Despite all the technical analysis that experts spout, the basis of the movement is two very human emotions — fear and greed. Investors fear they will lose money and sell stocks or they see an opportunity to rake in the bucks. This does not mean that every investor is greedy or fearful. It is just that these emotions tend to drive the stock market. After all, no one wants to lose money, and everyone wants to make money.

Fear and greed also drive the real estate market, but there is one other emotion involved — pride. By this, we mean pride of ownership. Every person who owns a home or other property has pride in it. The reason pride is mentioned is because it is an emotion that will need to be dealt with, particularly with residential properties. Because of pride of ownership, home owners will tend to overvalue their homes in negotiations. Investors cannot get caught up in their emotions. Remain objective and decide on the value based on a market analysis. Be sure to get a lease option on a house at a wholesale price, not a retail one. Otherwise, a profit will not be made. So make a low offer. If the seller takes the offer, fine. If he or she insists on a retail price, move on. The deal is not right then.

Let us now take a closer look at the primary values every real estate investor uses to evaluate potential investments.

UNIVERSAL DETERMINANTS OF VALUE

In any real estate market, there are four essential factors that determine the value of properties:

- **Demand** — The more people want a property, the higher the price goes.

- **Scarcity** — This is the supply/demand ratio. When properties are scarce, prices go up; when there is an oversupply, prices go down.

- **Transferability** — A clear title is absolutely essential to lease options or any other form of real estate transaction. If there is no clear title to a property, it is essentially worthless because it will end up in a time and money consuming legal entanglement at best or no sale at worst.

- **Utility** — The more uses a property has, the more potential it has for profit simply because there are so many more ways to sell it or the lease option.

In the previous chapter, we discussed the general forces that influence value — economics, physical forces, political, and social. Now let us get deeper into the subject by looking at specific factors that influence value.

SPECIFIC DETERMINANTS OF VALUE

The determinants listed below are ones that investors need to be very familiar with. They will guide decisions on whether or not to purchase a lease option.

- **Appraised value** — Value an appraiser places on a piece of real estate; the figure is usually at or near retail value.

- **Loan value** — Value a lender places on a piece of real estate; this figure often varies as a percentage of the appraised value.

- **Property tax value** — Value tax assessor places on a piece of real estate; the figure could be higher or lower than the retail value.

- **Replacement value** — Value insurance companies place on the improvements on a piece of real estate; the figure is determined by a cost approach.

- **Retail value** — The value an owner or end user places on a piece of real estate; this tends to be the highest value because of the pride of ownership factor mentioned earlier.

- **Wholesale value** — The value investors place on a piece of real estate; this tends to be the lowest value.

Once these six values are understood, the value of a specific property can be determined.

THREE METHODS OF VALUATION

There are three widely accepted approaches to determining the fair market value of a property: the *cost approach,* the *sales comparison approach, and* the *income approach*. Real estate appraisers will use one or more of these methods to determine the value of a property.

THE COST APPROACH

Basically, the cost approach method values two elements of a property — the land and the improvements on the land. It then determines the accrued depreciation of the improvements. This is then subtracted from the total value to arrive at the property value. Below is an example of how it works. An accrued depreciation of $50,000 is assumed.

Land value	$150,000
Improvements	+ $350,000
Total	**$500,000**
Accrued depreciation	– $50,000
Property Value	**$450,000**

Generally speaking, the cost approach method is most reliable when used on newer structures, but it tends to become less reliable as properties grow older.

THE INCOME APPROACH

This method analyzes the income a property produces in order to determine its value. The more income a property produces, the higher its value. Income can be figured in two ways. The first is the *gross rent multiplier* method. The formula looks like this:

Value = Gross Annual Rent x Gross Rent Multiplier (GRM)

Call a commercial real estate company or other source in the area to find out what the gross rent multiplier is. In the example below, we assume the gross annual rent is $150,000, and the GRM for the area is 7.

Gross Rent	$150,000
GRM	x 7
Property Value	**$1,050,000**

The second method to use is called the *income capitalization* approach and is a little more complicated. The formula looks like this:

Value = Income ÷ Capitalization Rate

In this method, the income is the *net operating income* (NOI). NOI is the gross income of the property minus the operating expenses. The market in which the property is located determines the capitalization rate. Again, this rate can be found by calling a commercial real estate company in the city and asking for the figure. Here is how the method works: Assume an investor is looking at a property and the NOI is $70,000 with a capitalization rate of seven percent. The property value would be determined this way:

NOI	$70,000
Capitalization Rate	÷.07
Property Value	**$1,000,000**

If the capitalization rate for the same property was eight percent, then the value would be lower at $875,000.

THE SALES (MARKET) COMPARISON APPROACH

The comparison method looks at the price or price per unit area of similar properties being sold in the marketplace. One property is compared to similar properties to determine value in terms of age, condition, amenities, time of sale, size, location, etc. Prices are then adjusted to account for differences. Let us use a single family home example to illustrate this practice.

An investor wants to know the value of a 1,500 square foot home with two bedrooms, two baths, and an attached two car garage. To find the comparable value, check similar properties that have sold within the past six months in the same neighborhood. For this exercise, we will assume there are two comparable properties. The first comparable property is 1,500 square feet, has two bedrooms, two baths, and an attached two car garage. It sold for $180,000 30 days ago. The second comparable home is 1,600 square feet, has three bedrooms, two bathrooms, and an attached two-car garage. It sold for $200,000 45 days ago. Calculate the cost per square foot for each of the properties by dividing the sale price by the square footage.

Here are the results: The first comparable property has a cost per square foot of $120 (180,000 ÷ 1,500). The second has a cost per square foot of $125 (200,000 ÷ 1,600). To estimate the value of the target home, take the lower square footage figure of the first comparable property and multiply by the square footage of the target home. The result is:

1,500 sq. feet
x $120
Value = $180,000

Of course, this is a preliminary figure. Do a walk through of the property to determine its actual condition. We will consider walk through evaluations in more detail in Chapter 10.

Be aware that there are different types of comparables and methods of recognizing value in the area(s) being targeted:

- **Appreciation rates** — These indicate the annual percentage increases in the market value of properties. They will provide an indication of how hot or cold the market is. Double digit appreciation rates say the market is hot, while single digit rates indicate it is good. A cold real estate market is shown in zero or negative rates.

- **Sold comparables** — This is the first method to determine value as shown in our example above. Basically, sold comparables set the base for the retail value of real estate. This category of comparables is useful for properties sold within the past six months. Any property sold beyond the six month time period is not considered a good comparable.

- **Listing comparables** — These are properties currently on the market which are similar to the target property. This category sets the upper limit for the retail value of real estate because they have not sold or closed escrow. They simply indicate what sellers would like to get for their properties.

- **Expired comparables** — These are properties that have never sold nor closed escrow. They show the value beyond the present market in terms of what buyers are willing to pay. Generally speaking, retail buyers will buy the lower priced comparable properties.

- **Pending comparables** — These are properties that have sold, but not closed escrow. They show the direction of value. When a pending comparable closes escrow, it then becomes a sold comparable. For example, if sold comparables are indicating a value of $150,000 and the pending comparables are showing a value of $158,000, then it indicates the value trend is headed upward.

- **New or planned developments** — As discussed earlier, this is the path of progress and serves as an indicator that properties in the path will appreciate in value.

- **Vacancies** — High vacancy rates may indicate problems with the property and/or neighborhood. Low vacancy rates indicate potentially profitable properties.

SOURCES OF FINANCING

Beginners in lease options will need to learn about and become an expert on sources of financing for lease options. Here is a brief summary of possible sources and the advantages and disadvantages of each:

Conventional Financing

This is the traditional approach to buying property. It is taken by qualifying for a new loan from a bank or mortgage lender. In most cases, there is a minimum ten percent down payment plus closing costs. Many people take this route because it provides the ability to purchase almost any property with a good interest rate. The disadvantage is that only so many of these loans can be qualified for. Banks and mortgage lenders are conservative by nature and they will balk if a person attempts to take out too many of these loans, particularly with single family properties.

Fixed Rate Unsecured Lines of Credit

These lines are issued through unsecured credit cards. If this route is chosen, seek out ones with fixed rate and low interest. An unsecured loan is made solely on the promise to repay. The lender will need to consider the investor a good risk. The best way to be considered a good risk is to have no debt and a very high credit score (in the top five to ten percent). The advantage of an unsecured line of credit is that, unlike a home equity loan, a person's house does not have to be put up as collateral and expensive closing costs charged by lenders do not have to be paid. One disadvantage is that, unless a person has zero debt and a high credit score, higher interest rates will likely be paid — defeating the purpose of getting such a line of credit in the first place. A second disadvantage is the temptation to over borrow and accumulate debt that is not needed.

Home Equity Loans

There are two types of home equity loans — closed end and line of credit. A *closed end loan* is similar to a home mortgage; that is, a specific amount of money is loaned out and scheduled monthly repayments of principal and interest must be made. Another way to look at a closed end loan is as a second mortgage. The date by which the loan must be repaid is set when the money is borrowed. Often interest rates are fixed. To obtain financing for lease options, choose the second type — a *home equity line of credit.* This option acts more like a credit card and allows a person to use as much or as little of the credit line as desired, up to an approved dollar amount. It has the advantage of allowing a person to withdraw money when they want to use it. Normally, a person has between five and twenty years to access this credit line. Once the period has ended, borrowing must be stopped and the principal and interest must be repaid. A typical range of repayment is between ten and twenty years. Or there may be balloon payments, which require the principal to be paid in one lump payment. Often, the credit interest rate is adjustable; that means the rate changes as the economy fluctuates. In general, home equity loans have several advantages. The rates tend to be lower than credit card rates or consumer loans. Such loans are also flexible. They allow a person to choose when to use the money. In addition, a person may be able to decide when to repay the principle. Another advantage is tax deductibility. The interest paid is tax deductible up to $100,000 or the equity value in the home, whichever is less. Check with a tax professional for details on the subject. Home equity loans also have disadvantages. There is a risk of losing one's home if the loan cannot be repaid or refinanced. That is because the home is collateral for the money being borrowed and is subject to foreclosure. Being late or missing loan payments can trigger foreclosure within 60 to 90 days. In that case, a person will be forced to sell or lose the home. Another disadvantage is the possibility of rising interest rates. If there is a variable rate, the monthly payments can rise or fall, depending on the economy. Most variable interest loans have "caps;" a cap sets how high the interest rate can increase each year as well as how much it can increase over the whole loan time period. Be sure to know what the cap is on the loan's interest rate. Finally, there are fees with home equity loans — origination fees application fees, withdrawal fees, etc. Be sure to find out what fees are being charged upfront so unnecessary expenses can be avoided.

Private Financing

Private financing can be found through an arrangement with investment partners. Generally speaking, this is not a strategy for beginners simply because they do not have the track record to impress potential investors. However, it is definitely a goal to aim for due to its advantages in buying lease options and property in general. First, due to the cumulate wealth of the investors, larger equity positions and can be acquired and thus properties that are potentially much more profitable. Second, the hassle of qualifying for loans from conventional lenders is eliminated. Third, closings are much less expensive, much easier, and definitely much quicker. Fourth, funds from retirement accounts can be accessed to buy investment property. Fifth, those who invest money from such accounts can typically get much higher returns than in certificates of deposit or money-market funds. Finally, foreign investors cannot easily qualify for loans in the United States so private financing gives them access to the market — and provides an additional source of funds.

Seller Financing

This occurs when the original owner of a property wants the investor to step in to help them. For example, if preforeclosure is in the works, they will want someone to take over the financing and the property and pay the arrears. This approach has several advantages. First, a new loan is not being obtained; the current loan is just being taken over and payments are being made. That means no loan fees or down payments. Second, time is saved since a new loan does not need to be applied for. Instead, the closing is relatively quick and cheap. The disadvantage of this approach is that many sellers will not agree to it. Seller financing is not as open a route as other methods.

INFORMATION SOURCES

The Internet is a wonderful source for information on both residential and commercial properties. Use data from the sources listed below to get a good and realistic idea of the value of properties being considered. Be sure to make use of them. Both the residential and commercial sources listed below are among the most prominent, but other sources can be found.

Online sources for Residential Properties
• DataQuick **dataquick.com**
• Domania **domania.com**
• HomeGain **homegain.com**
• HomeRadar.com **homeradar.com**
Online sources for Commercial Properties
• CoStar Commercial **costar.com**
• DataQuick **dataquick.com**
• Intelius **intelius.com**
• LoopNet **loopnet.com**
• IDM Corporation **idmdata-now.com**
• National Real Estate Index **graglobal.com**
• REIS Inc. **reis.com**

8

FINDING PROFITABLE DEALS

Investors in lease options deals have one purpose — to find undervalued properties that will turn a profit. To find these deals, be persistent and dig to find sellers. Undervalued properties do not just walk in the door. They are often below the radar. This chapter outlines several approaches that can be taken to locate these properties. Try any or all of them and keep the ones that work best.

ADVERTISEMENTS

Search for likely prospects in the newspaper, online, or in local real estate publications, or place ads to gain prospects. Make the ads short, sweet, and immediately readable. Do not start throwing in abbreviations. Readers do not always know what the abbreviations mean and often get annoyed at having to decode them. Here is an example of a simple, but effective, ad:

> Firm looking for 2–3 area homes for long term-lease.
>
> Call 123-456-7890

Ads like this are designed to draw in sellers who are considering long-term leases or individuals who want to rent out their homes. Try different styles of ads to see which ones draw the biggest and best responses. Beyond newspaper and Internet ads, do not forget publications like school directories, church fliers, etc. For a small price, these types of ads can support good causes and receive good exposure.

BIRD DOGS

"Bird dogs" or "scouts" can be a good source of inside information. Essentially, these individuals have a single goal — to find potential deals and then sell that information to other investors. They charge a fee for this service and the fees vary. It all depends upon the property price and its profit potential. A bird dog may make from $250 to $1,000 on each lead that ends with a purchase by another investor. Becoming a professional bird dog is a great way to get started in the real estate market because it does not require any cash on the bird dog's part or any previous knowledge in order to look at properties. It is also the fastest way for them to earn cash. The main requirements for becoming a bird dog are time, motivation, and the patience to do lots of searching. They will use a combination of the following search techniques to find properties:

- Post flyers at grocery stores, laundromats, or other locations with lots of foot traffic and high visibility.

- Check the newspaper real estate section for such ads as "Handyman Special," "Fixer Upper," etc.

- Advertise in the local newspapers and online. Or they run their own ads in the Real Estate Wanted section of the newspaper.

- Drive around and note houses in disrepair or properties that have become obsolescent.

- Some get jobs as property inspectors. This way, they get a good sense of the market and the properties that are available.

When working with a bird dog, make sure they know the goals and concentrate on the properties being looked for. In terms of "bird dogging," another, probably cheaper, course can be taken. Build a network of part time scouts; that is, individuals with full time jobs who are looking for extra cash. This network could include virtually anyone: business associates, coworkers, delivery truck drivers, dentists, doctors, employees, friends, mail carriers, neighbors, repair men, taxi drivers, tenants, trash collectors, utility meter readers, etc.

Business Cards

Have cards readily available at all times and hand them out. The cards should say specifically that a person buys or leases homes. Make sure that the contact information is printed on the cards — name, address, phone number, e-mail, Web site, etc.

Chamber of Commerce

The local chamber should have a list of businesses coming into or leaving town so it can be a good source of current information.

Corporate Relocation Departments

These departments often have an inventory of properties that have not sold. If there is no company corporate buyout policy, the property owners would likely love a lease option. After all, they have already relocated and do not need the added burden of making payments on two homes.

Direct Mail

Done properly, direct mail is an inexpensive and easy way to contact out-of-town and problem property owners in the area. All that is needed is a computer application that has mail merge capabilities (Microsoft Word,

WordPerfect, etc.) In the application, create a form letter which can then be merged with the appropriate names and addresses. Direct mail is also quick. Response will be received within two weeks' time. Plus, there are no third party hassles. In the letters, keep the offer simple, direct, and clear. Use the letter on the next page as a model to send to the owners of problem properties and revise it to meet needs. It can also be adapted for use with the owners of vacant properties.

Finder's Fees

Let people know that a finder's fee will be paid if they locate a property and the investor buys a lease option on it. Set the amount to pay, but it has to be attractive enough to entice people to locate properties. In his book, *How to Make Money with Real Estate Options*, Thomas J. Lucier says he pays $500.

Fliers

Post tear off fliers in any prominent public place that allows them — drug stores, grocery stores, convenience shops, etc. They should have the same information as in the newspaper ads. Make them attractive so as to draw attention to them.

FSBOs

This term refers to "For Sale by Owner" postings. Often referred to as "fizz-bos," these are owners who attempt to sell their properties without the aid of a realtor. They often find it is much harder than they think it will be and get overwhelmed by the process of dealing with buyers, lenders, title companies, and other parties involved in the market. This hassle can motivate them to sell quickly. A timely letter or call from an investor can relieve them of aggravation and create a win-win situation for both parties.

Direct Mail Sample Letter
Proposal to Buy a Real Estate Option

Date

Name

Address

City, State, ZIP

Dear Mr. Smith,

I would like to offer you a great opportunity on the property you own at 123 Oak Street in Anytown, (state). I would like to purchase a real estate option on this property. It would be under the following terms:

1. I will buy an 18 month option to buy your property as is for the option fee of $5,000. This amount will be credited toward the purchase price when the real estate option is exercised. The option fee is yours to keep, whether or not I exercise the option and buy the property.

2. When the real estate option fee is exercised, I will buy your property for $125,000 and close on the purchase within 30 days.

3. Upon exercise of the option, I will make a total down payment of $10,000. This will include a $3,000 credit for the real estate option fee paid.

4. When the real estate option is exercised, you agree to take back a first mortgage in the approximate amount of $115,000 at a 7.5 percent annual percentage rate with monthly loan payments based on a 30 year amortization period....(add appropriate information).

I am sure you will find this offer of great interest. To discuss the matter, please call me at (number) or e-mail me at (e-mail address). I look forward to hearing from you.

Sincerely,

(Name)

Multiple Listing Services (MLS) — Long-Term Listings

Consider hiring a realtor to search listings that are over 90 to 120 days old. These properties are taking too long to sell and the owners will likely be motivated to deal.

Out-of-State Owners

Many out-of-state owners live far away from their properties and find it a burden to deal with the issues involving those properties. Perhaps they inherited the property or had to relocate. These individuals can be found by checking with the county's property tax roll. It should list the mailing address for the parcel. Contact the county property appraiser or assessor's office to see if they keep a database of property owners who reside outside the county. Or contact a private company, like those listed in the previous chapter, that maintains a similar database of real property ownership records.

REAL ESTATE INVESTMENT CLUBS

Such clubs are a prime opportunity to network with other investors so it is wise to join one. Often, they have unsold properties they want to sell or know of properties not in their area. Beyond that, investors can expand their knowledge of not only lease options, but other aspects of real estate that may be of interest. Remember that networking is a two-way street — be prepared to give as well as receive information.

Vacant Properties

A vacant home or other property says that someone is making payments on a property that is not being used. This can be a burden on the owner, but it is an opportunity for an investor to create a win-win situation by taking the property off their hands. Write the owner a letter. If there is no response, try the county tax rolls or the post office.

Word-of-Mouth

Once a reputation as a fair and honest investor has been established, leads and deals will come.

Three more categories — realtors, landlords, and qualified sellers – are extremely important and we have chosen to treat them at length as separate subjects in this chapter.

REALTORS

It is a fact that realtors control most of the real estate market in any city. That means they have access to sellers investors might like to target. It pays to work with realtors. They do not always like to work with investors, however, because it is harder to lowball a property and get the deal through — and realtors like deals because that is how they get their commissions. However, they will always have properties that do not sell or ones the seller feels the realtor is not selling fast enough. These are properties where creative solutions provided by investors can help them out.

Generally speaking, it is easier to approach realtors with lease option opportunities during a buyer's market because they do not get a commission if a property does not sell or if the listing expires and ends up listed with another realtor. Sellers also put more pressure on realtors to sell their homes in a buyer's market. This opens the door for investors because the realtor has to come up with alternative solutions in order to satisfy his or her customer. It is in an investor's best interest to educate realtors on the benefits of lease options and build solid business relationships with them.

The type of realtor to work with is called a *listing agent* — the agent who lists the property for the seller. Listing agents work with the property owners and try to build a reasonably close relationship with them in order to establish the trust that will result, eventually, in a sale and a commission. Because they do build these relationships, realtors find that owners tell them many things. Owners are not afraid to speak their minds when the property does not sell or does not sell quickly enough. Beyond sticking with the realtor or changing to a different one, their options often come down to two choices — taking the property off the market or renting it. These are two options the realtor does not want to hear. However, in their minds, the lesser of two evils is renting the property, and that is where the lease option investor comes into the picture. When the realtor gives an investor leads and he or she purchases the lease option, they know they will get a commission and get it paid quickly. That is because the investor will front the commission money (the seller always pays it as part of the transaction) for him or her. A win-win situation is created — the realtor sells the listing, the seller sells the property, and the investor buys an investment with lucrative potential.

Before any of this can be done, willing realtors must be found and relationships must be built with them. The first part is easy — listing agents are listed in the real estate section of the newspaper or online. Or they can be found through the investor groups mentioned earlier in this chapter. Also, once a good relationship is established with one realtor, he or she can provide access to other agents. The second part — building relationships — is harder but absolutely essential. It will take time so be committed and persistent. Investors need to convince brokers and realtors of the benefits of working with them and be able to answer the most basic of all business questions: What is in it for me?

After determining which properties have been listed for more than 90 days, employ these basic tactics:

Letters to Realtors

The letter should briefly mention the property the investor is interested in and quickly emphasize the benefits of considering a lease option and of dealing with an investor. At the end of the chapter is a general example that can be used as a model.

Phone Calls to Realtors

It is always best to follow up a letter with a phone call. In a realtor's busy day, letters can get lost or misplaced. A phone call also establishes a much more personal connection than a letter. Given a realtor's schedule, it is likely that message will have to be left on their answering service. This forces an investor to be succinct and get the benefits message across quickly. Also, if the realtor has no interest in the first place, it means valuable time has not be wasted in a longer phone call.

Presentations to Realtors

This is a cost effective way of reaching several realtors at once in their office. To hold a presentation at the office, an invitation must be extended first. Such offices can be very busy places with many requests made to get on their meeting agendas. Cut through the clutter with a simple message: I can help you sell more of your listings. Ideally, the investor already has a contact within the real estate office that can assist in pushing the message through and get the investor on the agenda. If not, call directly and ask to speak to the broker or office manager. Introduce oneself, explain the purpose, and immediately emphasize the benefits of the lease option strategy. Tell them the presentation will be brief and not take up more than ten to fifteen minutes of his or her time. The phone call can be preceded with a letter, letting the broker know to be expecting a phone call. This gives the investor the opportunity to not only list the benefits of the presentation, but also to provide references and testimonials from satisfied clients. An appointment may not be obtained the first time, but be persistent and contact the broker on a regular basis. During that time, he or she may have changed his or her mind or the market may have changed in the investor's favor.

In order to achieve the goal of establishing profitable relationships with realtors, educate them on lease options during the presentation. They may not be familiar with the concept simply because it was not part of their training. As part of gaining their real estate license, they learned about seller contracts, fair housing, legal issues, state and legal standards, etc., not creative options for making sales. Do not walk into a presentation assuming that every agent knows what lease options are. Be prepared to explain the concept in clear but not condescending language.

To be effective during a presentation, be thoroughly prepared ahead of time. This is no time to improvise. The best way to get organized is to prepare an agenda. This will keep thoughts in order and allow a powerfully effective case to be made in the allotted time. Use the sample agenda at the end of the chapter as a model. To ensure that the presentation receives a positive response right from the start be sure to take a simple step — bring bakery goods. It is expected in many offices.

Once the presentation has been made and questions have been answered, it is likely that interested agents will offer leads. If not, it never hurts to ask in a polite way. Do not forget to follow up with realtors who have expressed interest. This is a crucial step. Real estate agents are very busy and talk to many people during the day. That is why they need polite reminders of the benefits an investor can provide them. Give them a call once a month or every other month, depending on their reaction to these calls. If business has not been done with a particular agent, simply say something similar to this:

> Hi, Kim! This is _____ giving you a call. You will remember that we met on October 15 at my presentation on lease options at your office. If you have sellers who are considering renting their homes if they do not sell soon, I would certainly love to work with you on finding a solution for their problem. Remember, when you work with me, you get your commission fast and in full. So, if you have some lease option prospects in mind, please give me a call at _____. Thanks.

If business has been done with a realtor, they will still need reminders — and probably appreciate them since they are getting help earning commissions. When calling say,

> Hi, George! This is _____. Hey, I just wanted to thank you for your business and let you know that I am looking for another lease purchase opportunity. If you have any sellers right now who would benefit from an option, please let me know. Give me a call at _____. Hope you have had a great week! Look forward to hearing from you!

Of course, the key in working with real estate agents lies in one's actions. Be ethical and honest in all dealings. In the first place, it is the right thing to do. Second, the realtors' reputations are on the line. Their success depends upon a good reputation. And, remember, realtors have a grapevine that spreads news faster than the speed of light. Once word gets out that a person is unethical, that individual is effectively done in the market. Also, remember that realtors control upwards of 90 percent of the market. The dumbest thing to do is treat them badly. It is important to keep one's word on every deal and keep them informed of what happens on every lead. Follow up and tell them what has been done with a lead; for example, tell them that the property has been looked at and whether or not there is any interest. If not interested, be sure to explain why; for example, tell them in nice terms that it does not fit the needs, but that the lead is certainly appreciated and others are welcomed. In some cases, the agent may know that the property is overpriced but will still want an offer from an investor. He or she can then show it to the seller to convince them to reduce their price to a realistic level and a sale. The investor does not end up with the lease option, but he or she helped the agent make a sale and the realtor will remember that. Think of it as an added value service that is an investment in a long-term relationship with the realtor.

LANDLORDS

There are different types of landlords and each are motivated to sell for a variety of reasons. One type is the amateur who has watched too many infomercials about an easy way to make millions. These individuals soon find headaches they never imagined — bad tenants, ignorance of state and federal laws, tax complications, etc. After a while, all they want is out. The second type is professional landlords who are retiring or are simply burned out. They may not need the money from the sale of their property or may not even want to receive it yet because they will incur a big capital gains bill if they do so. In cases like this, they would prefer to option the property to an investor and take advantage of the 1031 Tax Deferred Exchange law. This tax law allows a person to sell one property and buy another without incurring capital gains taxes. All the profits simply have to be reinvested into the next property or properties within a specific time line. The new properties have to be of equal or greater value. In this instance, the tax is deferred into the future, not eliminated. It is a win-win situation. See the end of this chapter for a primer on 1031 Tax Deferred Exchange Law. Those who decide to move beyond lease options into a buy and hold strategy will definitely want to take advantage of it.

Of course, landlords may need some convincing about the arrangement, especially if they are ignorant about lease options and their benefits. That is where a bit of good, old-fashioned selling technique comes in handy. As we stated earlier, the benefits should be stressed to the customer and the question *What is in it for me?* should be answered. Benefits answer that question. Typical benefits are: saving money, making money, more convenience, more security, less hassle, etc. Specific benefits for landlords in terms of lease options include the following:

- *No maintenance hassles.* Tell the landlord, "As part of the deal, I will assume the maintenance work. That means you will not be getting any more aggravating phone calls at all times of the night or day."

- *No showings.* Tell the landlord, "I will handle all showings so you do not have the inconvenience of taking time out your evenings and weekends to do them. You will be freed of considerable aggravation and have less stress in your life."

- *No advertising costs/hassles.* Tell the landlord, "I assume all advertising costs and will handle all calls regarding the property. Your time is your own again and you have eliminated a business expense."

- *Timely rent.* Tell the landlord, "With me, you get a monthly check every time, on time, regardless of whether or not the tenant has paid me on time. You have the security of knowing that this income is guaranteed every month."

- *Vacancies.* Tell the landlord, "I pay whether the home is vacant or not. Your rent is guaranteed."

Benefits like these can be a powerful inducement to a tired or retiring landlord. They will be willing to lease the property for less money. By negotiating a lower payment with the seller, the property can then be rented and a good cash flow can be obtained.

QUALIFIED SELLERS

Unqualified sellers can waste one's time and money and delay the identification of qualified and interested parties. It is in the investor's interest right from the start to qualify sellers. This can be done by first looking for two categories of sellers. The first is individuals who do not need the cash out of the home to move on. The second is individuals who do not have any equity in their property. They have 100 percent financing. We will deal with the second category in this section. Generally speaking, these types will be found:

- **Inheritance sellers** — These are individuals who have inherited a property and who do not want the complications of maintaining and/or marketing that property. Through a lease option, they can be relieved of these complications. One caution: Limit these transactions to situations where there is only one or two inheritors. The more inheritors, the thornier the deal can become because of the usual family entanglements.

- **"Veteran" home owners** — By "veteran," we mean owners who have owned their property for a long time. Often, they are financially stable, have low monthly payments, and have a good savings cushion. This means they can buy a new home without selling the old one. This situation enables the investor to get a lower payment as well. The result is good cash flow.

- **New home builders** — These individuals have built a new home, but their old property has not sold yet. They do not want to pay for a vacant property. If the old home does not move quickly, they become more anxious to get it off their hands. They are motivated sellers — ideal candidates for a lease option.

- **Recently married individuals** — In cases like this, the seller may have moved into their spouse's home and they certainly do not enjoy paying for property that is vacant. A lease option is a win-win for everyone involved. The seller is relieved of the burden of paying for the original property and the investor is dealing with an individual who had the financial capacity to pay for that property. Responsible people are being dealt with.

- **Transferred individuals** — We have mentioned this type earlier, but it bears repeating here. Transferees — especially those who are now out-of- state — may be anxious for a lease option because they do not want the burden of double payments. They may also like a lease option because they simply do not know how long the job will last or if it will work out at all. There is a lot of anxiety and an investor can help reduce or eliminate that anxiety by offering them a lease option.

There is a common characteristic among all these types — low debt. This means the investor avoids dealing with individuals who have financial difficulties and can be risky choices for lease options.

Human beings are being dealt with, many of whom have pride of ownership, so they cannot be expected to accept a lease option on the spot. Many will require persuasion and that is where salesmanship comes in. We stated earlier that an investor should emphasize benefits in any conversation with a prospective seller or buyer. This concept is so important that we will emphasize it here once again. Keep the following slogan in mind every time a customer is contacted:

People Buy BENEFITS!

A simple but effective sales step can be used in every contact. Here it is:

Step 1: Introduce yourself.

Step 2: Explain the reason for the call.

Step 3: Stress benefits.

Step 4: Ask for acceptance.

Step 1 is obvious. In Step 2, introduce the concept of a lease option and be prepared to explain what the concept entails. Remember not every one knows what a lease option is. If it is not explained, the prospective customer may be confused and lost. A simple way to find out if they understand the concept is to ask, "I would like to discuss a possible lease option on your property. Are you familiar with lease options?" Their answer will guide the conversation. After the explanation, proceed with Step 3 and introduce the benefits with statements like, "A lease option will reduce the stress of having to make payments on your vacant home." Once the benefits have been explained, take Step 4 and ask for acceptance. By acceptance, we do not mean asking the prospect to accept a lease option on the spot. It can happen, but it is unlikely. Instead, we mean ask them to agree to a meeting so lease options can be further explained and so the investor can get a look at the property. All these steps should be presented in a friendly and professional tone. The underlying objective is to establish a good rapport with the prospect.

When making these calls, understand that resistance may be encountered for various reasons. Often resistance is simply a natural reflex; they do not know who they are speaking with and are not about to commit until they are sure about the investor. They may say things like, "I am not interested," "It sounds too complicated," or "I do not think I would get a good bargain out of this deal," etc. Be prepared to handle this resistance; otherwise, you will miss out on some good deals. Use the following technique to handle objections:

Step 1: Acknowledge the objection, but do not agree with it.

Step 2: Offer counterbalancing benefits.

Step 3: Ask for acceptance.

For example, assume that a prospect is being spoken with and he responds by saying, "Well, I do not think I would be getting enough money out of the deal." Respond by saying:

"I understand how you might feel that way. However, remember, with a lease option, you will be rid of all those maintenance headaches, plus you will not have the burden of making payments on a vacant home. In addition, you will have the security of getting a guaranteed payment from me every month. When you consider all those benefits, how does a lease option look to you now?"

In the above statement, the objection was acknowledged without agreeing with it. Then, counterbalancing benefits were offered and finally acceptance of those benefits was asked for. This strategy does not work every time, but it will work consistently, especially if it is practiced diligently and adapted to one's personal style. It is a strategy many successful salespeople in all walks of business have used over the years.

Sample Letter to a Realtor

Name

Address

Phone number

E-mail

Fax

Dear ___,

I am writing concerning the listing you have on 567 Main Street. I see that it has been on the market for more than 90 days and I was wondering if your sellers would like to consider some creative options for their property. Specifically, I was wondering if they would be interested in a lease option arrangement. This is a wonderful solution for both you and the sellers. If they do not need to get their cash out immediately, it means they can get their monthly payments covered and be relieved of that burden. It also means you get your full commission paid much more quickly. It is a win-win situation. Please give me a call. My number is _____.

P.S.. If a lease option will not work for this seller, please consider this strategy for any of your other sellers who have indicated that they may have to rent if their property does not sell soon. Again, please call me. You do not want to lose your commission to a seller who wants to rent!

Thanks for considering my offer.

Sincerely,

(Name)

Sample Agenda for Realtor Presentation

I.   Introduction (name and name of company)

II. Purpose — to discuss lease options as a creative selling option

III. Benefits:
  A. Increase sales of listings
  B. Establish a mutually profitable relationship
  C. Explore alternative sales approaches

IV. What Type of Seller is Perfect for the Lease Option?
  A. Sellers whose properties are moving
  B. Buyers, etc.

V.   The Elements of a Lease Option
  A. Basic explanation
  B. How you earn a commission
  C. Seller benefits
    a. Payments taken over
    b. Maintenance taken over
    c. No rental problems
  D. Listing agent benefits
    a. Saves time and money through quick sale
    b. Commission is paid upfront

VI   Types of Properties I Look For

VII. Price Range Acceptability

VIII. Referral Fees

IX. Summary

X.   Question and Answer Period

A PRIMER ON TAX-DEFERRED 1031 EXCHANGE LAW

As mentioned earlier in the chapter, an investor will most likely want to take advantage of the 1032 if, at some point, he or she decides to move beyond lease options and into a buy and hold strategy. This tax law permits an investor to sell one property and buy another without incurring capital gains taxes. All that needs to be done is to reinvest all the profits into the next property or properties within a specific time line. It is important to remember, however, that the property must be qualifying property. This means property held for investment purposes or used in a taxpayer's trade or business. Investment property includes real estate, improved or unimproved, held for investment or income producing purposes. Real estate must be replaced with like kind real estate. "Like kind replacement property" can be any improved or unimproved real estate held for income, investment or business use. Here are some examples:

- Improved real estate can be replaced with unimproved real estate and vice versa.

- A 100 percent interest can be exchanged for an undivided percentage interest with multiple owners and vice-versa.

- One property can be exchanged for two or more properties.

- Two or more properties can be exchanged for one replacement property.

- A duplex can be exchanged for a fourplex.

- Investment property can be exchanged for business property and vice versa.

An investor cannot, however, exchange a personal residence for income property and income or investment property cannot be exchanged for the personal residence.

There are three types of 1031 tax deferred exchanges that can take place:

- *Straight exchanges* — Two parties trade properties of equal or approximate value.

- *Multiparty exchange* — This involves three or more parties buying, selling, or exchanging properties. These exchanges tend to be complex, and a tax professional will be needed for the process.

- *Delayed exchange* — This method allows the sale of the relinquished property and the buying of the replacement property to occur at different times as long as stringent rules are followed. This is the exchange most often used.

Note that, in these exchanges, the capital gains tax is deferred, but not eliminated. However, deferral is a wonderful way to leverage small real estate holdings into larger ones. Because gains can be postponed, a tax-deferred exchange strategy can be used to transfer equity to a larger property — all without paying taxes. Additionally, there is no limit on exchanges. This means, for all practical purposes, that a person can make as many exchanges as desired. This provides a profitable, long-range strategy. Over the course of one's lifetime, he or she can continually grow income and appreciation by adding new properties without having to pay the capital gains tax. This strategy is especially effective for those specializing in buying and renovating properties who want to keep reinvesting their profits into larger properties. If this is not, a person risks being classified as a real estate dealer by the IRS and will not be able to participate in exchanges.

Here are the basic rules that must be followed in order to qualify for a 1031 exchange:

- The properties to be exchanged must be located in the United States. A foreign property can be exchanged for a foreign property and domestic for domestic. However, these exchanges cannot be mixed together.

- Only *like kind* real estate can be traded.

- An exchange must be made that is equal to or greater in both value and equity. Any cash or debt relief received above this amount is considered "boot" and is taxable. *See explanation below for specifics.

- The *like kind* property must be identified within 45 days of the closing on the initial property.

- All proceeds from the initial sale have to be turned over to a "qualified intermediary," who is the person or company that plays the role of middleman. Any of the proceeds not under the control of the middleman are subject to taxation. The middleman holds the funds from the initial property in escrow until the closing on the second property occurs. The middleman also assists the owner with the preparation of paperwork and other services to ensure the transaction progresses smoothly.

- The closing on the second property must take place within 180 days following the close on the first property.

A note on "boot:" In order for a Section 1031 exchange to be completely tax-free, boot cannot be received. Boot is a word that is not in the Internal Revenue Code or Regulations. However, it exists, and it usually has this definition: Boot received is the money or the fair market value of other property received by the taxpayer in a 1031 exchange. *Money* includes all cash equivalents plus liabilities of the taxpayer assumed by the other party or liabilities to which the property exchanged by the taxpayer is subject to. *Other property* is property that is not like kind. This includes personal property received in an exchange of real property, property used for personal purposes, or non-qualified property. *Other property* also includes such things as a promissory note received from a buyer. Any boot received is taxable to the extent of gain realized on the exchange. Boot can be but is not always intentionally received and can result from a variety of factors. That means it is important to understand what can result in boot if taxable income is to be avoided. The most common sources of boot include the following:

- **Cash boot.** This is taken from the exchange and is usually in the form of "net cash received," or the difference between cash received from the sale of the relinquished property and cash paid to acquire the replacement property or properties. Net cash received can result when a taxpayer is trading down in the exchange so that the replacement property does not cost as much as the relinquished property sold for.

- **Debt reduction boot.** This occurs when a taxpayer's debt on replacement property is less than the debt which was on the relinquished property. Debt reduction boot can occur when a taxpayer is trading down in the exchange, the same as with cash boot.

- **Sale proceeds.** These are monies used to service costs at closing which are not closing expenses. If the proceeds of sale are used to service non-transaction costs at closing, the result is the same as if the taxpayer received cash from the exchange and then used the cash to pay these costs. That means it is wise to bring cash to the closing of the sale of a relinquished property to pay for the following non-transaction costs:

    o Rent prorations
    o Utility escrow charges
    o Tenant damage deposits transferred to the buyer
    o Any other charges unrelated to the closing

- **Excess borrowing.** If more money is borrowed than is necessary to close on replacement property, this causes cash being held by a middleman to be excessive for the closing. Again, excess cash held by a middleman is distributed to the taxpayer, resulting in cash boot. All cash being held by a middle man for replacement property must be used. Additional financing must be no more than what is necessary, in addition to the cash, to close on the property.

- **Loan acquisition.** This refers to costs with respect to the replacement property which are serviced from exchange funds being brought to the closing. Loan acquisition costs include origination fees and other fees related to acquiring the loan. Taxpayers usually take the position that loan acquisition costs are being serviced from the proceeds of the loan. However, the IRS and the lender may take the position that these costs are being serviced from exchange funds.

- **Non like kind property.** This is received from the exchange, in addition to like-kind property. Non like- kind property could include such items as seller financing, promissory notes, etc.

Only the net boot received by a party is taxed. In determining the amount of net boot received, certain offsets are allowed and others are not, as follows:

- Cash boot paid (replacement property) **always** offsets cash boot received (relinquished property).

- Debt boot paid (replacement property) **always** offsets debt reduction boot received (relinquished property).

- Cash boot paid **always** offsets debt reduction boot received.

- Debt boot paid **never** offsets cash boot received (net cash boot received is always taxable).

- Exchange expenses (transaction and closing costs) paid (relinquished property and replacement property closings) **always** offset net cash boot received.

These rules are complicated and a tax advisor should be on top of them. However, here are some general rules regarding the boot.

- Always trade across or up. Never trade down. Trading down always results in boot received — either cash, debt reduction, or both. The boot received can be mitigated by exchange expenses paid.

- Bring cash to the closing of the relinquished property to cover charges which are not transaction costs.

- Do not receive property which is not like-kind.

- Do not over-finance replacement property. Financing should be limited to the amount of money necessary to close on the replacement property in addition to exchange funds which will be brought to the replacement property closing.

All in all, a 1031 exchange is a wonderful tool for deferring taxes. However, keep in mind that it also has risks. For example, it can be difficult to complete the purchase agreement within 180 days in a highly competitive market. If that happens, a taxable transaction will result. Another negative is that the exchange includes a reduced basis for depreciation in the replacement property. The tax basis of replacement property is essentially the purchase price of the replacement property minus the gain which was deferred on the sale of the relinquished property as a result of the exchange. To put it another way, the replacement property includes a deferred gain that will be taxed in the future if the investor cashes out of the investment. A third disadvantage is that the investor may chase deferred capital gains so hard that he or she ends up overpaying for a property and more taxes on it in the future.

9

DUE DILIGENCE — YOUR SAFETY NET

Once likely sellers for lease options have been identified, the work has only begun. A close examination of the property is always in order — no matter how good it looks. Seldom do properties come without problems. Some are minor and easily repairable at low cost; some are hidden and can represent major expenses. Whether checking information on the Internet, over the phone, or in person, be sure to examine closely any public records on a potential lease option property and verify the information in them. The records are not always accurate. The most up-to-date information possible is desired to avoid any problems. Let us look at Internet searches more closely this resource can maximized and used effectively.

INTERNET SEARCHES

The first step in using the Internet is to do a search. Sometimes it is as simple as entering the property owner's name into the window. If they have done something unscrupulous, then their name may pop up in court records. More often, it is a case of accessing local records and digging into the information available there. Once on the Internet, there area many places to find information about a specific property. The first stop is the local county property appraiser/assessor site and other appropriate sites listed below to find out the following information:

- **Code violations** — Look for code violations cited for the targeted property by the local code enforcement agency.

- **Comparable sales** — The county property records should show sales of comparable properties during the past six months. This will provide an idea of the current worth of the property.

- **Crime search** — Determine the crime risk rating for the property's address with the local law enforcement agencies.

- **Demographic information** — Check all demographic data to see what the makeup of the neighborhood is.

- **Flood zone map search** — There should be federal flood maps available. Check the maps carefully a flood-prone area is resided in.

- **Hazardous waste search** — Avoid any property with hazardous waste issues since clean-up can be extremely expensive. Check the records carefully for any evidence of environmental hazards. Any violations could be on local, state, or federal agency sites.

- **Property records** — Examine the county property assessor/appraiser's property records to find out information on ownership, sale, tax assessment information, etc.

- **Property tax records** — Search the country tax collector's property tax records for information on tax payments.

Of course, there are many other sites to check for more specific information on topics. Here are several:

CRIME STATISTICS

- The Disaster Center — **http://www.disastercenter.com/crime/**

- NeighborhoodScout — a subscription site **http://www. neighborhoodscout.com/neighborhoods/crime-rates.jsp**

There are many other sites on crime available on the Internet. A search will find more.

DEMOGRAPHIC INFORMATION

- ESRI — business information solutions (**http://www.esri.com/ data/index.html**)

- Federal Financial Institutions Examination Council (FFIEC) Geocoding System (**http://www.ffiec.gov/Geocode/default. aspx**)

- U. S. Census Bureau
  - **http://quickfacts.census.gov/qfd/index.html**
  - **http://www.census.gov/cgi-bin/gazetteer**

ENVIRONMENTAL HAZARDOUS WASTE

- Department of Housing and Urban Development (HUD) — HUD has environmental maps available (**http://egis.hud.gov/ egis/**)

- Environmental Protection Agency (EPA) (**http://www.epa.gov/ superfund**)

- Enviromapper (EPA) — search by zip code (**http://www.epa. gov/enviro/sf**)

- Scorecard.org — information on pollution and environmental hazards (**http://scorecard.org/**)

PROPERTY RECORDS

- National Association of Counties — **http://www.naco.org**

- Property Reports (Intelius) — **http://find.intelius.com/property-check.htm**

- PublicRecordFinder.com — **http://www.publicrecordfinder.com**

- Searchsystems.net — **http://www.searchsystems.net**

Many more such sites are available online; do a search to find them. Be sure to double check information with the local government offices to make sure there are no code violations, tax liens, environmental hazards, etc. These agencies may have up-to-date information that has not yet been placed on their Web sites. Some areas may not have the county property records available on the Internet. In that case, call the customer service department at the property appraiser/assessor's office. Give them the property's street address. With that information, they should be able to provide:

- Parcel or folio number

- Owner's name and mailing address (if it is different from the property address)

- When and how much the property last sold for

- Current tax-assessed value

Those who are more hands-on can always visit the county offices and do a title search to determine if there are liens, etc. Most likely, the record books and/or microfiche files will be used. Owners of vacant properties can also be located through this method. However, sometimes this information is missing or incorrect. If that is the case, check the following sources:

PROPERTY OWNER NAMES

To find names, check with the county property appraiser/assessor. Nearly all names are on the tax rolls. The roll lists every parcel of land within a given county. The tax identification numbers will vary according to the office's regulations. They could either be an assessor's parcel number (APN) or an appraiser's folio number. To find out if the county's tax roll is online, type the county and state information into the search engine window.

Sources for Locating Vacant Property Owners

County

- Business license records
- Jail inmate records
- Public library patron records
- Voter registration records

State

- Bar association records
- Department of Motor Vehicles records
- Fishing/hunting licenses
- Professional license records
- Prison inmate records
- Vital statistic records

Federal

- Prison inmate records
- Social Security Administration (death index)

As part of the search, look very, very closely at two areas to make sure there are no problems — liens and titles. Let us look at these areas next.

LIENS

Under U.S. law, a lien is defined as "any sort of charge or encumbrance against an item of property that secures the payment of a debt or performance of some other obligation." Another definition is "a claim against an item by another party which utilizes that item as security for repayment of a loan or other claim. A lien affects the ability to transfer ownership." The last sentence is important to investors in lease options. If ownership cannot be transferred, a lease optioned property will do an investor no good at all. It is important to be aware of the types of liens that are out there so "liened" properties can be avoided. Liens can be voluntary (mortgage or trust of deed lien) or involuntary (the result of legal action). Information about liens can be found at the following sources:

- **Circuit court office** — Check for tax liens on state income, state inheritance, state franchise taxes, etc. Also, check for liens against estates of deceased persons, guardianship of minors and incompetents, termination of joint tenancies, etc.

- **County clerk's office** — Same as above.

- **Country recorder's office** — Look for judgment liens, property tax liens, federal tax liens, etc. Check for conditional sales contracts (contracts for deed, land sales contracts, etc.) In addition, look for notices of "lis penden." This is a notice filed or recorded for the purpose of warning all persons that the title or right to the possession of certain real property is in litigation. The Latin term literally means "suit pending."

- **Municipal clerk's records** — Analyze the records for any liens for failure to pay for municipal services like water, sewer, and trash removal services. Also, check for any code enforcement fines.

- **United States Court** — Look for any federal judgments against the title holder. These could include federal tax liens and liens resulting from defaults on FHA, Department of Veterans Affairs (DVA), SBA, and student loans.

Common types of liens are shown at the end of the chapter. Become familiar with all of them so a thorough search of records can be done. One last note on liens: If there are several liens on a property, they are generally treated by the law in chronological order. In other words, a lien recorded on June 1 would have priority over a lien recorded on June 15 of the same year. However, liens for unpaid government services may have priority over other liens in several states. It is best to check with the local and state governments to find out what the rules and regulations are.

TITLES

Of course, clear and free titles to any properties being lease optioned are desired. That means a title search is extremely important. There are two common types:

- *Current owner* — This is a search of public records from the date the property's title was transferred to the present owner to the current date.

- *Full title search* — This is an exhaustive search of the property's title from the date the current owner gained the title back into the past (up to a maximum search of 60 days).

Undertaking a title search is definitely an area for a professional title abstractor or title examiner because it can be very complicated and tricky. To find a professional examiner/abstractor, check local sources or go online to The National Association of Land Title Examiners and Abstractors (**http://www.naltea.org/**) and use their directory.

INSURANCE CLAIMS

Always check a property's casualty and property insurance claims history before buying a lease option on that property. Determine if it is insurable and insurable at a reasonable rate. Insurance rates are expensive so it pays off in the long run to verify the claims history. On the Internet, check with CLUE (Comprehensive Loss Underwriting Exchange). CLUE, which can be found at (http://www.choicepoint.com/business/pc_ins/us_3.html), is a database of consumer claims created by ChoicePoint, a leading provider of decision-making information and technology that helps reduce fraud and mitigate risk. It is a database that insurance companies insurance brokers can access when they are underwriting or rating an insurance policy. A CLUE report includes the following information:

> "...policy information such as name, date of birth, and policy number, claim information such as date of loss, type of loss, and amounts paid, and a description of the property covered. For homeowner coverage, the report includes the property address and for auto coverage, it includes specific vehicle information."

Have an insurance broker check this information to make sure the property is definitely insurable and insurable at prevailing rates for similar area properties.

PROPERTY DISCLOSURE AGREEMENTS

An investor may want to make sure he or she is doubly protected by having the property owner sign a property disclosure agreement before a lease option is purchased. The agreement should be one approved for use by the state. Have the owner sign the statement in the presence of a notary public. Agreements will vary by state, of course, but generally ask questions in the following areas:

- Property defects

- Environmental hazards

- Pest control problems

- Legal problems

- Title

- Zoning problems

If such questions are not asked on the state form, be sure to ask them.

All of the above efforts need to be backed up with a physical inspection of the property. In general, the investor or an inspector should be looking at the following areas:

- Code enforcement

- Condition of properties within the neighborhood

- Crime rates

- Good availability of municipal services.

- Public nuisances

- Public perception of the area

- Storm water drainage

- Traffic patterns

The next chapter will treat physical inspection in more detail.

Common Types of Liens

Bail bond lien — A bail bond allows a person arrested on criminal charges to be released on a bail pending his or her trial. One way to get a bond is to pledge capital on the form of real property.

Child support payment — When a property owner fails to make court ordered child support payments, the state government places a lien against the property's title.

Code enforcement lien — This type of lien occurs when a property owner has been fined for failing to correct the code violations and has failed to pay the resulting fine. The local enforcement board then places the lien on the property's title.

Corporate franchise lien — This lien can occur within states that have a corporate franchise tax for the right to do business within those states. If a corporation fails to pay the tax, the state places a lien against any corporate real property within the state.

Federal judgement lien — This lien concerns debtors who have defaulted on federally guaranteed loans. When default occurs, a lien is placed against the property title.

Federal tax lien — When a person fails to pay federal income tax, the Internal Revenue Service has the statutory power to place a lien against the title of any real property belonging to that person.

Homeowner's association lien — This lien can occur when a member of a homeowner's association fails to pay their dues as per the deed to the property. The lien is placed against the property title.

Judgement lien — This type of lien occurs when lawsuits award monetary damages to the plaintiff. In this case, a lien is placed against both personal and real property of the defendant until judgement is placed.

Common Types of Liens

Marital support lien — When a property owner does not pay court-ordered marital support, a lien is placed against a property's title. This can be done on the local, state, and federal levels.

Mechanic's lien — This is a statutory lien which allows architects, contractors, engineers, mechanics, surveyors, etc. to take legal action against a debtor who has failed to pay for furnished work or material for the improvement of real property. The lien is placed against the real property being worked on.

Mortgage and deed of trust lien — This is a voluntary lien created when real property is pledged as security for the repayment of the debt.

Municipal lien — When a property owner fails to pay for municipal services, the local government places a lien against the property's title.

Public defender lien — When a property owner fails to pay for a court-appointed public defender, governments place a lien against the property title.

Real property tax lien — When a property owner fails to pay his or her property taxes, liens are placed against the property by local authorities.

State inheritance tax lien — This is a tax levied against the estates of deceased individuals. If the tax is not paid, a lien is placed against the estate for the amount owed.

Welfare lien — When a property owner fraudulently collects welfare payments, the local, state, and federal governments can place a lien against the property's title.

10

PHYSICAL INSPECTION OF THE PROPERTY

Unless an investor has construction knowledge and experience, it is highly recommended to hire a professional building inspector to do a detailed inspection of any property that is being considered for a lease option. Do an inspection as well to get a sense of the property as a lease option investment. If problems are obvious and the property is not a good investment, then the expense of a professional inspection has been saved. However, if that is not the case, then definitely go with a professional. There are simply too many ways that unscrupulous owners can hide defects, and repair of these problems can cost a considerable amount of money. Just think of the damage that can be caused by out-of-date or defective water pipes, not to mention rotting roofs, dry rot, mold, termites, and bad wiring. If a property inspector does find problems, require the seller to correct those problems or reduce the price. If they do neither then consider walking away from the deal before any damage is done to your personal finances. As mentioned previously, many states protect an investment by requiring that a seller provide a disclosure statement. Generally speaking, sellers are responsible for disclosing only information within their personal knowledge. Some states, however, do specify certain problems that the seller must take responsibility to search for, whether or not they see indications of the problem. Check with the state to find out if this is the case. If so and a seller willfully avoids mentioning the defect, take him or her to court for compensation. Finally, if an owner tries to limit access to a property, walk away from the deal. He or she may be trying to hide problems.

FINDING A BUILDING INSPECTOR

Check locally to find out which licensed building inspectors are highly regarded. Never go with an unlicensed inspector, especially if the state has no standards for this profession. It is wise to interview a minimum of two or three inspectors before choosing one. Be sure they are full time professionals conducting a minimum of 50 to 100 inspections per year, depending on the area. Ask inspectors for copies of their recent written inspection reports. If they do not want to share them, run the other way. Any professional wants to show samples of his or her work. Also, be sure to ask for a minimum of three references. The references should be clients who have used the inspector's services within the last six months to a year. Contact them and get their opinions on the inspector's work and behavior. Once a choice has been made, go along with the inspector on the first tour of the property. The investor will not only see how this person works, but will also have the opportunity to learn the specifics of inspection.

We recommend going with The American Society of Home Inspectors (http://www.ashi.org/) or the National Association of Home Inspectors (http://www.nahi.org/). Members adhere to a code of ethics in a profession where they are sometimes lacking due to fly by night operations. Members are also forbidden to have a professional interest in the sale, repair, or maintenance of a property they inspect. They also cannot use their inspection business as a way to find customers for a handyman service that they happen to own. Use ASHI's "Find a Home Inspector" link to identify candidates in the area. Home inspection rates vary by inspector, region, and size of the house. According to **Bankrate.com**, approximately 40 percent of buyers pay in the range of $200 to $250. Survey local inspectors to find out what the rates are in the area.

WHAT IS INVOLVED IN A BUILDING INSPECTION?

The building inspector should do a *physical or structural inspection.* A property that is not structurally sound is not desirable. Here is a list of questions that should be asked so the investor is armed with the knowledge of what information a property inspector should provide:

- What property repairs are needed?

- Which areas (if any) are unsafe or causing rapid and expensive damage?

- Are there priorities for repairs? If so, what are those priorities?

- How should repair priorities be adjusted for my circumstances?

- What repairs may cost me a lot of money?

- What are the biggest risks of hidden damage?

- Are there inexpensive alternative repairs? If so, who is available to make these repairs at a reasonable cost?

- Are investigations into other repairs appropriate?

In more specific terms, a professional inspector should be examining the following areas (listed in alphabetic order):

- Electrical System Wiring, Service Panel, Devices, and Service Capacity

- Energy Conservation / Safety Items

- Exterior Walls, Siding, Trim

- Floor, Wall, Ceiling, Roof Structures

- Foundation, Footings, Crawl Space, Basements, Sub-Flooring, Decks

- Gutters, Downspouts

- Heating and Cooling Systems

- Insulation and Ventilation

- Interior Floors, Walls, Ceilings

- Moisture Intrusion / Mold

- Overall Structural Integrity

- Plumbing Systems (fixtures, supply lines, drains, water heating devices, etc.)

- Property Drainage / Landscaping

- Roof, Roof Shingles, Chimneys, Attic

- Walks and Drives

- Windows, Doors, Cabinets, Counters

When a walk through is done, there may be obvious signs of damage. Look for the clues shown on the following pages using a checklist to check off defects so they can be kept track of.

All in all, it pays to be extremely thorough when inspecting a property. It also pays to be extremely methodical when qualifying a seller or buyer of lease options. That is the subject of the next chapter.

COMMON HOUSING DEFECTS

☐ **Bad floors** Slanting or sloping floors can be a sign of serious problems with the foundation or the quality of construction. Also, check for soft spots on upper floors. This can indicate structural damage.

☐ **Cracks** Look around the foundation, walls, ceilings, windows, door frames, chimneys, and retaining walls for cracks. If a seller tells you that these are "subsidence" cracks, do not accept this story at face value. It may or may not be true. The only way to find out is to let a professional do an inspection. Otherwise, use this rule of thumb: If a crack is big enough to stick the width of a pencil into it, then something more serious than subsidence is likely occurring.

☐ **Evidence of moisture damage and/or presence of mold** Mold can be particularly dangerous to the health of inhabitants. It can cause allergies, infections, irritations, and toxicities. It can also be very difficult and expensive to get rid of, so you definitely do not want it present in any building you're considering. Mold has a characteristic musty smell, so check for that odor. In terms of moisture intrusion (snow or rain), look for discoloration and stains on ceilings and walls and around windows and door frames. These clues may indicate serious structural damage. Also, look for sump pumps. They are specifically designed to handle flooding in basements and lower levels. If you find them, have the inspectors check the property out in detail.

☐ **Grounds** Some soil problems can be very expensive to fix, so look for evidence of poor drainage, excess groundwater, or cracks in the foundation. Do not forget to check the drains. They should all be correctly installed and maintained.

COMMON HOUSING DEFECTS

❑ **Out-of-true structure** Modern technology is a wonderful aid in determining if a structure is out-of-true. Laser levels are available at inexpensive prices and are definitely worth the cost. Using such a level, walk through a property looking for floors, walls, and ceilings that are not in plumb. Do not forget to open and close doors and windows as well. If they stick, you know things are not in line.

❑ **Pest control inspection** Depending on the part of the country, pests can include termites, carpenter ants, powder post beetles, and any other bug that likes wood. These insects can cause very serious damage to a property. Also, look for dry rot and other similar fungi. It is best to bring in a professional pest control operator to identify any of these problems.

❑ **Plumbing leaks** Internal leaks can do a considerable amount of damage, so check all potential leak sources sinks, faucet lines, toilets, dishwashers, washing machines, sprinklers, etc. Special note: Avoid any property with polybutylene domestic water supply systems. Due to its tendency to gradually deteriorate through interaction with chlorine and other chemicals in drinking water, it has been the subject of class action lawsuits over the years. The most widely known brand name was Qest (manufactured by Shell Oil Company). It was a very popular type of pipe used in residential and commercial installations in the 70s and the 80s. Indoors, polybutylene pipe is gray colored and flexible. When used in a yard, it is blue colored. In terms of overall plumbing, it was used for both hot and cold plumbing.

11

DOING THE NUMBERS — EVALUATING PROFITABILITY

Assume a good deal has been found for a lease option. The first thing to do is to keep a cool head. Do not rush into the deal. It is time to crunch the numbers. "Doing the numbers" means determining what the profit goal is. For example, if the goal is a $20,000 profit, then that is the bottom line number; any less will not be accepted. If the deal will earn only $15,000, then there is a choice. The terms can be negotiated to meet that requirement, or the deal can be walked away from. Of course, negotiation is an art, not a science, so that means an investor can get creative and work with a seller or buyer to reach the bottom line. Let us look at specific ways in which profitability can be evaluated and a good decision can be made.

FACTORS IN EVALUATING PROFITABILITY

A worksheet will be needed to evaluate all the factors involved in lease option deals. Please see the example on the following page.

Purchase Costs	
Purchase price	
Total purchase costs	
Income Sources	
Current value	
Value of lease option premium (5–10%)	
Projected appreciation	
Projected sale price	
Expected monthly cash flow	
Total other income	
Projected Profit	

Some of the elements on the worksheet will have to be estimated. Here is how to do that.

APPRECIATION

Appreciation will vary from location to location. Do some legwork to find out if it is acceptable for the property in mind. Newspaper articles are one source. Another source is the local realtor community. Consider running a test ad in the paper. The number of responses will determine if the price is too high or too low. In other words, if too many responses are received, the price is probably too low. If there are too few, then the price is too high. A rule of thumb is to use five percent appreciation in areas where the properties are consistent in size, model, etc. If the neighborhood is more varied, use an appreciation rate of up to ten percent.

CASH FLOW/RENTAL VALUES

To find these values, use the comparable method discussed earlier in the book, but use it to determine rentals instead of sales. Again, read the paper and check out all the local rentals. Also, contact individuals in the local landlord organization(s).

Now, let us plug in some numbers using a case study. Assume a seller will give an investor a lease option on a home for $190,000. The current market value is $200,000 and the appreciation rate is five percent per year. The property will be sold on a 24 month option. This will result in ten percent appreciation (two years x five percent = ten percent). This gives the investor $20,000 of appreciation during the two years ($200,000 x 10 percent). The owner will be paid $1,500 in monthly rent. It will then be rented out for $1,800 which provides a cash flow of $300 per month. Now, assume the property is in a diverse neighborhood with prices ranging from $175,000 to $300,000. Because of this, an option premium of ten percent of $20,000 is built in. This means the $20,000 option premium and $20,000 appreciation adds $40,000 to the retail value of the home (now $240,000). The completed worksheet looks like this:

Purchase Costs	Case Study	
Purchase price	($190,000)	($190,000)
Total purchase costs	($190,000)	
Income Sources		
Current value	$200,000	
Value of lease option premium (10%)	$20,000	
Projected Appreciation	$20,000	
Projected Sale Price	$240,000	$240,000
Expected monthly cash flow (24 mos x $300)	$7,200	
Total other income	$7,200	$7,200
Projected Profit		**$57,200**

If all payments were made and the option went the full 24 months, the profit would be about $57,200, less transfer fees, title insurance, option credits, etc.

If that is the profit target that was aimed for, then the deal is right. If not, then continue negotiations or turn the deal down. Note: Try to build in added profit to cover unexpected expenses.

In addition, use the worksheet to determine the profitability of "subject tos." Remember that this area is similar to lease options. The difference is that a loan balance will be taken over and perhaps liens, back taxes, etc. The profitability determining process is a little more complicated, but essentially the same as with lease options.

On the next page there is a case study. In this example, the sellers owe $150,000 on their first mortgage and $25,000 on their second. Between the two mortgages, they are behind $3,110. They have no other liens on their home and the property taxes and insurance are up-to-date. The home is presently worth $188,000 and is situated in a market with six percent annual appreciation. The diverse neighborhood has homes ranging from $155,000 to $260,000 so the option premium is set at ten percent. Monthly payments for the first mortgage are $1,075 and $225 for the second mortgage (total = $1,300). The home will rent for only $1,200 monthly, resulting in a negative cash flow. This is a result of the sellers having two mortgages (higher payments) and poor credit (higher interest — higher payments). During the option period, the principal portions of the mortgage payments are approximately $258 per month or $3,100 for 12 months (258 x 12 = $3,096). When the home was bought, the escrow received from the seller was $1,800. The projected profit is $42,770. If that is the profit being sought, then this is a good deal. Remember that this is a "subject to" cash will be needed upfront to do the deal – $3,110 — plus there will be a negative monthly cash flow of $100. If it is not a good deal, negotiate or move on to a better deal. Negotiation is a large part of buying and selling lease options and is the subject of our next chapter.

Purchase Costs	Case Study 2	
Purchase price Total purchase costs		
Purchase Costs		
Balance owed on 1st mortgage	($150,000)	
Balance owed on 2nd mortgage	($25,000)	
Upfront cash requirement for back payments and total liens	($3,110)	
Total debt on property		($178,110)
Income Sources		
Current value	$188,000	
Lease option premium value (10%)	$18,000	
Expected appreciation (6%)	$11,280	
Expected sale price	$217,280	$217,280
Expected monthly cash flow (-$100 monthly for 12 months)	(-$1,200)	
Additional principal from mortgage	$3,100	
Payments during option period		
Escrow balance	$1,800	
Other income	$3,600	$3,600
Projected Profit		**$42,770**

12

NEGOTIATING

———

Investors in lease options are also salespeople. It is necessary to convince sellers and buyers of the benefits of dealing with an investor in order to make negotiations go as smoothly as possible. And that means the ability every effective salesperson has needs to be developed — the ability to create rapport. Because it is so important, let us look at this subject in more detail.

BUILDING RAPPORT

Rapport is defined as the "relationship of mutual understanding or trust and agreement between people." Earlier, we discussed the importance of emphasizing benefits with sellers and buyers of lease options and with realtors and landlords. That is definitely part of rapport; however, building trust goes beyond that. Whenever possible, it is all about building personal connections with people. It is about showing interest in their personal situation. A connection can be built with most people through simple methods.

First, be natural and do not adopt high pressure sales tactics by pointing out all the faults in a property. Do not forget about pride of ownership. Look for items that can help build a personal connection. Perhaps, a husband is a golfer or a fisherman and has photos of these activities on the walls. If the investor is also a fisherman, it never hurts to say, "I see you like fishing, too. My favorite spot is Meadow Lake. I have gotten some good catches out there.

How about you?" In this case, the investor and the husband have a hobby in common and it serves as a good icebreaker. Never lie about hobbies or awards and claim to be involved in them when it is not the truth.

Second, once the individuals have opened up a bit, simply ask them why they are interested in a lease option for the property. Ask them in a nice way with an open question such as, "What are your goals for this property?" Before going any further, read the primer on open questions in the following graphic to understand why they are so important.

A Primer on the Use of Open Questions

Open questions are ones that encourage a person to open up and expand on a subject. Often they begin with words like, "What," "Why," "How," "In what way," or "Tell me more." This is a time-honored sales step and it is effective. Here are some examples:

- How do you feel about a lease option?

- In what ways do you see the property being used?

- What are your plans for the house?

- Why are you interested in selling an option on your property?

- Tell more me about your reasons for considering a lease option.

Of course, once general information has been gathered, closed questions can then be used to gather specific information. A closed question is one that simply asks for a "yes" or "no" answer, as in, "Do we have a deal?" "Are the terms acceptable?" "Does the home have any liens on it?" However, at the beginning of a conversation, stick with open questions. Those are the ones that will help in building rapport.

A third tactic to use is to recognize the personality of the seller/buyer and match it in a subtle way. People have different personalities. Some are extroverts, individuals who are friendly and outgoing and outward directed. Some are introverts and are quiet and inward directed. Others are analytical and demand a reason for everything. They tend to be objective, cool, and calm. Keep in mind that no one is only one type. We all are mixtures of these types. Also, realize that there is no need to get overly involved in analyzing a person for his or her type. Often, an immediate sense of a person can be gathered upon meeting them. What is important is to match their style in a subtle way.

Basically, we all feel more comfortable with individuals who are like us in terms of interests, speech, temperament, etc. The technical term for this is mirroring and it can be an effective technique for building rapport. It makes use of a subtle conversational technique in which the gestures and habits of the person being talked to are reflected. Mirroring works because it is based on human psychology. When we see someone who acts like us, we automatically think they are similar to us. That makes us feel comfortable or friendly toward them. If a conscious effort is made to reflect back to customers the type of person they are, they will feel comfortable. Generally speaking, a person's behaviour can be mirrored in four areas:

- Gestures (body movements, handshake, etc.)

- Posture (how the person sits, legs crossed, etc.)

- Voice (volume, pitch, speed, rhythm, inflection, etc.)

- Breathing (are there many pauses in the person's speech or few?)

For example, if the person uses a lot of sweeping gestures, do the same. If their voice is quiet and controlled, speak in the same manner. Of course, be subtle about the whole process. Do not make individuals feel as though they are being made fun of.

Fourth, and perhaps the most important skill of all, is the ability to listen. It is a vital element in building rapport and in closing the deal. One reason for its importance is that sellers do not expect salespeople to listen to them. A second reason is that listening allows a person to pick up clues and information as to what sellers are thinking and how they are feeling. That allows the salesperson to tailor the presentation to meet the particular needs of those individuals. The result is more closed deals. Much has been written about listening, but there is no need to get technical about the skill. Follow the basic guidelines below.

Basic Listening Guidelines

- **Focus on the person**. Give your full attention to the seller/buyer. Maintain eye contact. Do not look out the window or at what else is going on in the room.

- **Do not interrupt.** Sometimes you can be too eager to get on with the deal and want to prod the owner into action by interrupting. This is a mistake. Always let the seller or buyer finish before you begin to talk. Everyone appreciates having the chance to speak without being interrupted. When you interrupt, you are telling them that what they have to say is not important and you definitely do not want to give that impression.

- **Use prompts.** If you want a seller or buyer to keep talking, nod your head while they are speaking or use verbal prompts like, "I see," "Go on," "Tell me more," etc.

- **Use summaries.** Often, you can make sure you understand what a seller is saying — and keep them on track — by providing a short summary of what they have said. This gives them the opportunity to either expand on what they have said or correct any misunderstandings on your part. A summary can be as simple as, "So, what I hear you saying is that the property has been vacant for too long but you are concerned about the kind of tenants I might bring into your house."

Finally, avoid the mistake that many individuals in the real estate business make, particularly real estate agents. They trot out statements like "I sold a million dollars worth of property last year," or "I did a hundred deals last year," or "My company is the biggest in the area." Customers simply do not care that a person has sold many properties or bought a lot of lease options. All they want to know is, "What can you do for me personally?"

NEGOTIATING SKILLS

Much has been written about the skills of negotiation. But, for lease options, it does not have to be complex. First of all, if benefits are emphasized, negotiations will be much easier. The question, "What is in it for me?" will have been answered before the negotiation process is started. Second, use the following general guidelines to build on those benefits during negotiations.

Guideline 1: Prepare thoroughly. Always think through what is wanted out of the deal before meeting with an owner. If this is not clear, things can end up in a muddle or the deal can be lost. Before negotiations even begin, answer the following questions:

- What is the maximum amount I am willing to pay for this real estate option?

- What is the maximum amount I am willing to pay for this property?

- What terms am I willing to accept in the option agreement?

- What terms am I willing to accept in purchase of the property?

Make sure to study the area and property closely, crunch the numbers, and have a good idea of the seller's needs. Make sure you know what cycle the market is in. For example, if it is a seller's market, an investor will likely have to buy higher., and if it is a buyer's market, be sure to buy below the retail value because the appreciation rate might not be favorable or not there at all.

Remember to stick to the objectives. If a property that is 20 percent below market value is being sought, then negotiate to achieve that objective.

Guideline 2: Be professional in appearance and actions. We all know the old expression: "You do not have a second chance to make a good first impression." Making a great first impression is the gateway to winning over an owner and smoothing the path to obtaining a lease option. Dress professionally and conservatively to create an aura of solidity and trust. Do not arrive for a meeting dressed casually or sloppily. At best, this creates a bad impression and makes the job of selling the owner on the benefits of a lease option much harder. At worst, the owner will automatically write the investor off and the discussion will be short and unprofitable. Also, act professionally. Treat the owner with respect and let him or her know that the investor is acting in their best interests. Not only will most owners appreciate professionalism, but they will spread the word to their friends and neighbors, potentially creating more business.

Guideline 3: Determine what the owner knows. Not all owners know what a lease option is. Determine the extent of their knowledge from the beginning and be prepared to explain the concept and its benefits. Keep it simple and clear. No one likes to be baffled by real estate jargon. Such jargon creates confusion and suspicion in owner's minds, making the purchase of a lease option much more difficult. Find out how owners arrived at their estimate of the property's market value. They may have an unrealistic estimate. If they do, then present the income and sale analysis and demonstrate to them that it is all verified. This will bring a dose of reality to negotiations.

Guideline 4: Create a win-win situation. Do not enter negotiations with a "win at all costs" mentality. The objective is not to make the owner feel like he or she has been bested in negotiations. Instead, the objective is to make the owner feel like he or she is a partner in the process and both sides have won.

Guideline 5: Listen. It is a fact that the best negotiators are often quiet listeners. They encourage owners to talk first and listen patiently while they make their case. Good negotiators never interrupt because they know they are gaining information that can be useful when it comes time to discuss numbers.

Guideline 6: Ask for commitment. If an investor does not ask, he or she will not receive. If a good job of offering benefits has been done and the deal meets the owner's needs, ask for commitment to that deal. Here is a simple, but effective way to ask for commitment:

Asking for Commitment
Step 1: Summarize the seller's needs
Step 2: Summarize the benefits that meet those needs.
Step 3: Ask for commitment

Here is an example:

> *"Kim, you have said that you do not want the burden of mortgage payments on your vacant property and are looking forward to having the stress out of your life. With this deal, I assume the mortgage payments, and you get rid of the stress. I will also make sure nice tenants move into the house who will take good care of it. This deal works for both of us, wouldn't you agree?"*

In the above example, the speaker summarized needs, and then summarized the benefits that meet those needs. The speaker also threw in an extra benefit — nice tenants. Then, the speaker asked for commitment.

All of the above guidelines are easy to learn and they can be made a natural part of one's delivery through practice. Be like an athlete who hones his or her skills on a daily basis. With consistent practice, this will be a natural and effective method of negotiating with sellers and buyers of lease options.

HANDLING RESISTANCE

Resistance from some owners who may feel that a lease option is not a good deal will be encountered. This is a natural part of the selling process so it pays to be prepared to handle resistance. It usually takes two forms — doubt or objections. A doubt means someone is not sure about the deal or about the investor for various reasons. Doubt is heard in statements like:

"I do not know if this is a good deal or not."

"I am not sure I want to go through with this."

"How do I know you will treat me fairly?"

The main way in which to handle a doubt is to offer proof. The model is similar to the handling objections model described earlier in the book. In the graphic below, notice that only the second step is different.

Steps for Handling Doubt

Step 1: Acknowledge the doubt, but do not agree with it.
Step 2: Offer proof.
Step 3: Ask for acceptance.

Offer proof in the form of numbers, testimonials, or years of experience. For example, assume an investor is talking with an owner who says, "I have never dealt with lease options before. How do I know you are legitimate and not some fly-by-night operation?" Answer the doubt this way:

"I understand your concern. I brought along testimonials from satisfied customers in the area. I would like you to look them over. I also brought their phone numbers and urge you to contact them. As you will see, I have a pretty good client list. That is the result of ten successful years in the business. So, when you look at my solid track record and my list of local clients, how do you feel about working with me now?"

Of course, this model can be adapted.

The other form of resistance — objections — was covered earlier, but here is a brief refresher before we cover some of the specific doubts and objections that will likely be encountered during the course of business. The model for handling objections is this:

Steps for Handling Objections
Step 1: Acknowledge the objection, but do not agree with it.
Step 2: Offer counterbalancing benefits.
Step 3: Ask for acceptance.

Again, the model can be adapted. Practice it until it is a smooth and natural part of the delivery.

TYPICAL FORMS OF RESISTANCE

It is likely that one or more of the scenarios listed below will be encountered. We have provided answers to each of those scenarios which can be used as models for the basis of other responses.

Situation 1: "I do not know. I do not want tenants in my home who might not take care of it."

Answer: "I hear what you are saying, but there is no need to worry on that account. Remember, I want to put a tenant in who is going to be future home buyer. They will have a vested interest in good upkeep of the property. Also, remember, it is in my best interest to screen tenants carefully, and that is exactly what I do. In fact, I have a list of satisfied tenants right here."

Situation 2: "I am not sure about this part of the lease option where it says you do not have to exercise the option. What happens if you do not exercise it?"

Answer: "I can understand your concern, but I want to assure you that in case I do not exercise the option, the property will revert back to you. And not only does it revert back to you, but I will make sure it is in the same great condition or even better condition. I will also give you 30 days' notice so you will have to plenty of time to consider other alternatives."

Situation 3: "I am uncomfortable with what might happen if you do not make the mortgage payment. I could be left holding the bag."

Answer: "I hear you, so let me address your concern directly. First, I can provide you with references from other sellers. When you talk to them, you will find out that I am always reliable in terms of meeting mortgage payments. Second, when I make the mortgage payment each month, I will mail you the receipt. That way, you have proof positive that I am making the payments. How do those solutions work for you?"

Situation 4: "Why will it take you so long to buy the home? That seems like too much time."

Answer: "I understand your feelings on the subject. It takes about 18 to 24 months to finalize a deal. That is because, sometimes, tenant-buyers come and go. However, remember, it is my best interest as well as yours to make sure I find the right buyer and do everything carefully and correctly. In fact, it is my job to help them through the whole process, and I will do exactly that."

Situation 5: "I do not think you are putting enough money down on the option. Why will you not put down more?"

Answer: "I hear what you are saying. The reason I am not putting more down is that I incur more risk since I do not actually own the property. Also, it limits my ability to purchase more homes and help others to move into homes they would really like to have."

Resistance will vary with the individual owner. However, if the models for handling doubts and objections are learned and practiced, resistance can be successfully overcome in any situation and many sales will be closed.

UNDERSTAND WHAT YOU ARE NEGOTIATING

An investor has to be clear on the definition of a real estate option agreement, not only for himself or herself but also for potential sellers of options. Sellers will be encountered who either do not know what an option agreement is or are fuzzy on exactly how it works. In basic legal terms, here is how such an option is defined: It is a unilateral agreement, binding only on the seller (optionor) in which a promise is exchanged for performance. In other words, the promise is the exclusive, unrestricted, and irrevocable right and option to purchase. This is exchanged for the performance — the exercising of the option by the buyer (optionee). The purchase of the option does not impose any obligation on the buyer to exercise the option and purchase the property. In plain English, it means that the buyer has the option in hand and can buy or not buy the property within the specified time period. Once the option is exercised, the agreement is no longer unilateral. It becomes bilateral and binding on the optionee and the optionor. At this point, the optionee becomes the buyer and the optionor becomes the seller.

Also understand the essential, basic elements that make up a real estate option agreement. The first is a stipulated real estate option period; that is, a buyer has the right to exercise the option within a specified amount of time (12 months, etc.) The second is a clearly defined method of exercising the option. And the third is valuable consideration paid as an option fee by the optionee. All of these elements must be in compliance with the state's real property statutes. Do not download an option agreement from the Internet and assume that it meets the laws of the state. What is legal in California may not be legal in New York. It is a basic tenet of our justice system that ignorance of the law is not a valid legal defense. Avoid potential law suits, court dates and/or out-of-court settlements by making sure the agreements are fully legal in the state. Use an attorney to prepare and review all documents. See "Safeguard Yourself and Your Investments" later in this chapter.

Once in the process of negotiations, be very clear on what items are included in the lease option agreement. In alphabetical order, key items to include are listed on the next page. Keep in mind that there are many other stipulations that can be negotiated in lease option agreements. There are so many that they cannot all be listed here. The best course is to educate oneself completely on the subject through study of the local market and conditions. Also, keep in mind that the inclusion of stipulations has one purpose — to limit the risk!

There are additional areas in which a buyer can negotiate to reduce the price — repair costs, code violation citations, operating expenses, etc. These will vary with the property so be sure to inspect each one closely to see what those areas are. Also, keep in mind that in some situations, it may be necessary to ask the sellers to pay part of the payment. This happens when owners have taken all or most of their equity out through means of a second mortgage. Usually, these mortgages come with higher interest rates and higher monthly payments. If this is the case, ask them to continue to pay the second mortgage for a specified period of time until the property is resold or the appreciation catches up.

KEY ITEMS

- **Assignment of real estate option agreement** — Stipulate the right to assign or sell the agreement to a third party during the option period.

- **Credit for option fee** — Unless there is a different arrangement, stipulate that the option fee can be credited toward the purchase price when the option is exercised.

- **Escrow for title transfer documents** — Stipulate that a warranty or grant deed and purchase agreement be held in escrow by an attorney or title/escrow company during the option period. Make sure the documents are notarized.

- **Extension of option period** — Negotiate for the right to extend the option period for set amount of times (e.g., two three-to-six month periods). This should include the cost of each extension period.

- **Fixed purchase price** — Be sure to negotiate the fixed purchase price of the property. This should include the down payment amount and the terms of financing.

KEY ITEMS

- **Length of the real estate option period** — Choose a period that is most advantageous.

- **Memorandum of real estate option agreement** — Stipulate the right to record a memorandum in the official public records.

- **Property entry right** — The buyer definitely wants the right to enter the property so it can be cleaned, fixed up, showed, and marketed.

- **Property clean up credit** — Stipulate a cleaning credit that can be applied toward the option fee for cleaning up the property.

- **Purchase price of the real estate option** — Negotiate an option fee that does not exceed a set percentage of the property's current market value.

- **Refund of option fee in case of damage or destruction** — Natural disasters can occur, so stipulate a full refund of the option fee if the property incurs damage or destruction from earthquakes, fires, thunderstorms, etc.

- **Refund of option fee for eminent domain action** — Negotiate that a full refund of the option will be received (plus any accrued interest) if the property is condemned by eminent domain during the option period.

- **Sole remedy for default** — Stipulate that the option fee paid is the exclusive remedy in the event that the real estate option is exercised but the property is not purchased.

SAFEGUARD YOURSELF AND YOUR INVESTMENTS

Lease options can be a legal minefield. One wrong step and a profitable investment can be destroyed. It is absolutely essential to engage the services of an experienced, board certified real estate lawyer to review all documents before a deal is signed. A good attorney can save considerable time, money, and trouble, so his or her fee is definitely money well spent. Ideally, seek out attorneys who have considerable experience in preparing lease option agreements in the state. Of course, be sure to check qualifications and references. To do this, first contact the local or state bar association referral service. Then, do an online search of the state bar association membership to find out if the attorney is licensed to practice law in the state. Also, check to see if there are any references to disciplinary actions for misconduct. If a nationwide search for attorneys needs to be conducted, use one of the following sites to search for information on them:

- **FindLaw.com** — click on the "Research a Lawyer" link

- **Lawyers.com**

- **LegalMatch.com** — click the on "Real Estate and Housing" link

Once lawyers have been located, talk to several to find out which ones can explain lease option agreements in plain English rather than in legal terms. It will be easier to work with them because they are good communicators. Finally, make sure they are associated with a reputable title insurance firm and are licensed to sell title insurance in the state. Be sure to take these steps:

- Make sure all documents are properly witnessed.

- Keep a master copy of all documents.

- Hold all property title transfer documents in escrow. Including:
    - One copy of the witnessed and notarized real estate option agreement
    - One copy of the real estate purchase agreement
    - One copy of the warranty or grant deed
    - Two copies of the buyer and seller's closing costs (HUD 1 Settlement Statement or other appropriate documents)

Of course, double-check all documents for mistakes before signing.

13

CLOSING

———

Once all the skills have been successfully employed and all the techniques described in the previous chapter have been followed, the reward of closing has then been earned. If the advice in Chapter 12 was followed, then the closing should go quite smoothly because all the details of the transaction have been worked out and finalized before sitting down at the table with the owner. All that needs to be done is to have the optionor sign the appropriate documents in the presence of a notary. There are always exceptions, of course. Some optionors will attempt to play hardball and try to increase the price of the option fee. If this is the case, simply tell them that negotiations have been made in good faith and the terms already agreed upon should be abided by or the deal is off. This tactic usually brings them around quickly.

In regard to signatures, it is important to remember that they must be properly witnessed by a notary. Otherwise, they may not be enforceable in court. The same is true of other property title documents. If they have not been properly notarized, they cannot be recorded in the county's public records.

Also, have a board-certified attorney present at the closing. Contrary to common notions, title and/or escrow agents are not objective participants committed to making sure all dealings are fair. They look out for the interests of the title insurer or escrow company. That means the buyer needs to have someone there to represent his best interests and that person is the attorney. Also, keep in mind that many title and escrow agents are used to dealing with conventional sales and may not be all that knowledgeable about lease option purchases. In some cases, they may regard the buyer and the deal with a certain amount of suspicion. The presence of an attorney will give them a better level of comfort with the closing process and make it go more smoothly than if the buyer were the only person at the table.

To keep everything legally clear, provide specific, detailed written instructions to the attorney or title or escrow agent acting as the closing agent and holding the title transfer documents in escrow during the option period. Make sure the joint escrow instructions are witnessed and signed by both parties and notarized. Make a list of all documents to be held in escrow during the option period. In addition, be sure the escrow instructions specify exactly what is going to occur when the real estate option is assigned, extended, exercised, or will expire.

A "memorandum of option" is recommended. This document is a record against the title of the property. It lets the public know that the buyer has an interest in the property. The purpose of recording the memorandum is to prevent an unscrupulous seller from refinancing and selling the property to someone else. An example of a memorandum is provided at the end of the chapter. Recording the memorandum and not the actual option agreement is recommended for two reasons. One, the terms should be confidential, and, two, you do not want to let the competition know what is going on.

14

ADVANCED STRATEGIES

There are more advanced techniques that can be practices once the basic strategies of lease options and subject-tos have been learned. They are designed to take an investor to the next level — the level of increased protection and profitability. They are more complex and, thus, require more studying.

ADDING PROTECTION

The memorandum of option is a means of protecting an investment. This option is reliant upon the "good faith" performance of the seller holding the title to the property. Most sellers do exactly that; they meet the terms of their legal obligation. However, there will be times when "bad faith" sellers who are determined to squirm out of their obligations will be encountered. Here are some techniques to head off these unethical people.

The Deed in Escrow

Escrow often refers simply to the deposit of funds by one party for the delivery to another party upon completion of a particular condition or event. However, it also includes the deposit of deeds and other written financial/legal instruments. We recommend placing the deed in escrow at the time the memorandum of option is filed. In this case, the seller signs the deed along with the other contracts, but the deed is not recorded on the title at this point. Rather, it is held in escrow by a title company or attorney, and they are provided with instructions for its release. In terms of filing liens, this move does not protect the title against such action; however, it tends to reinforce to sellers that they have actually sold the property and, thus, creates a reluctance on their part to try to back out on the lease option agreement. It also has another advantage: It allows an investor to close on the property without the seller being present. With the deed in escrow, specify how and when the deed is to be released and recorded. The instructions can be a simple statement similar to this one:

> "When John Jones pays $200,000 in certified funds to Sam Smith, the deed will be released to him. By (date), these funds must be paid."

Performance Mortgage

In essence, this technique has the seller pledge the property as collateral for the lease option agreement and ensures good faith performance by the seller. Once the mortgage is assigned to the buyer, it prevents the seller from selling the mortgage to other people. It replaces the memorandum of option filing. The performance mortgage permits the seller's insurance company to put the buyer's name on the owner's policy as another insured. It also shows that the buyer is a lien holder and requires that he or she be notified if any type of foreclosure action is taken. Be aware that some sellers will not like the idea of a performance mortgage and refuse to take that course. Rely upon personal judgment of the person and the situation. As always, have an attorney review the terminology of the mortgage to make sure the appropriate, specific clauses are included.

Land Trust

A land trust is defined as:

> "…an organization established to hold land and to administer use of the land according to the charter of the organization. A land trust is a

useful way to manage complex divisions of the Bundle of Rights that people can own in real estate, and can be used to manage something as large and complex as a multi-state REIT [Real Estate investment Trust], or as common and small as a single family home."

Source: Investor Dictionary.com
http://www.investordictionary.com/

This technique can be used with subject-tos and seeks to minimize possible exposure to litigation. In essence, it hides true ownership because the actual owner or beneficiary is not recorded in the public records, only the name of the trust. This means potential litigants find it difficult to identify someone to sue. Land trust contracts tend to be complicated and long. However, Wendy Patton, in her book *Investing in Real Estate with Lease Options and "Subject-To" Deals*, provides an overview of the key elements that should be included in any land trust contract. Her section on key mortgage clauses is good to familiarize yourself with prior to any investment deal.

Partnering

In some instances, an investor may want to consider subject-to properties that are high end (in terms of rapidly appreciating value) and, therefore, more of a risk. This is a time to spread that risk by taking on the seller as a partner. In this deal, the buyer and the seller share the profits. For example, assume a property is worth $800,000 and the monthly rental is $3,500. In normal circumstances, this deal would be backed away from. However, this home might be sold for $200,000+ in profits. This deal makes good financial sense and can be a win-win situation for both the buyer and the seller. An agreement can be entered on an equal (50-50) basis or negotiate a different percentage arrangement. If this course is decided on, then require that the seller cover all the risks.

Refinancing

This is a tax deferment strategy. In this case, assume a person has a house worth

$300,000 and only $230,000 is owed on it. Through a new mortgage, a person can take out some or all of the $70,000 in equity, and it is not a taxable event. That means a person can use that money to reinvest in other properties while still holding on to the original property. Check with mortgage brokers in the area to find out what refinancing programs are available. They will be able to tell a person what is available and appropriate for his or her situation.

Of course, with any of the methods described in this chapter, Internal Revenue Service (IRS) regulations will have to be met, so make sure that the investor and the CPA or tax attorney are on top of them. IRS regulations do change and can affect the legality and profitability of your deals. In particular, one area to be concerned with is capital gains. Capital gains are the profit on the sale of a property. At present, a person can sell his or her primary residence (the one actually lived in, not investment properties) every two years. If a person is single, he or she can keep the profits up to $250,000; if a person is married, he or she can keep up to $500,000. In both instances, the profits are tax free. If the seller of a property lives in his or her home for two out of five years, that property qualifies for a tax free gain. The seller can rent the home out for three years — and not a single day more. Many sellers may have little or no idea of what capital gains are. If that is the case, it is an ethical duty to educate them on the subject, particularly those individuals who have lived in their homes for long periods of time. Here is an example: Assume a widow has lived in her home for over 30 years and she has $225,000 in capital gains. If a buyer decides to purchase her house with three years of signing the lease option deal, it fits within the IRS guidelines — she pays no capital gains taxes. However, if the IRS limit as described above is exceeded, she will end up paying taxes and that could cost her a considerable amount of money. In this instance, it is the buyer's ethical obligation to inform her of the IRS rules and the consequences of not meeting them. If the capital gains are high, the best course would be to advise her to talk to a CPA and/or tax attorney before entering into a lease option deal. Remember, specific tax advice cannot be given (unless a person is a Certified Public Accountant), but customers can be steered onto the right course. It is the ethical and moral thing to do and will burnish one's reputation as an honest business person.

15

MAXIMIZING THE APPEAL OF THE PROPERTY

———

It takes no time to maximize the property's appeal to potential buyers. This is a vital step because it brings several benefits. First, it makes the property more attractive to buyers. Curb appeal allows an investor to make the best possible first impression upon passersby interested in the property. It also increases the number of interested parties, allowing the investor to pick and choose among potential customers and sell more quickly. Second, it discourages riff raff from damaging the property and decreasing its value. Vandals, drug dealers/addicts, squatters, arsonists — they can all wreak havoc on an investment or, in the case of arsonists, destroy it completely. Third, it increases the resale value — and the return on the investment. Maximizing appeal is a cost effective means of turning a profit.

By maximizing appeal, we do not mean that major rehab has to be done on the property or expensive investments in items like replacing appliances have to made. What money should be spent on is clean up and cosmetic improvements. This will cost a modest amount of money, usually anywhere between $500 to $1,500, depending on the size of the property. On the next page is a basic checklist of items to be done to maximize appeal. In addition, once the tenant has moved in, a video walk through of the property with that tenant during check in is recommended. Get verbal agreement that everything is in order and also have them sign the checklist. This serves two purposes. One, it protects the investor against any damage inflicted upon the property by the tenant and provides proof in case the investor has to go to court to recover damages. Two, it also protects the tenant against any unwarranted claims for damage. And, when a tenant moves out, be sure to change the locks to protect against any potential liability. Depending on the property, it can be stipulated as part of the lease option agreement that the tenant is responsible for maintenance and repairs. That, of course, will be subject to negotiations.

Maximizing Property Appeal Checklist

- ____ Remove trash from grounds and building
- ____ Mow grass
- ____ Remove brush, weeds, dead trees, etc.
- ____ Trim trees, hedges, etc.
- ____ Thoroughly clean the house/building
- ____ Pressure wash exterior of house/building
- ____ Pressure wash sidewalks, drive ways, etc.
- ____ Paint exterior/interior, if necessary
- ____ Carpet cleaning, if necessary
- ____ _____
- ____ _____
- ____ _____
- ____ _____
- ____ _____
- ____ _____

To keep costs to a minimum, it is best to budget right from the start and keep a checklist of expenses. An example is provided at the end of the chapter.

If an investor does not have time to maximize the appeal of a property, consider hiring the services of a professional to do the clean up. Often, a local person who is retired and is looking for part time work can be found. Ask around to find out which ones have a great reputation for doing quality work at reasonable prices. Once a person becomes more involved in the business, he or she will gain greater knowledge of these individuals and can make use of their services. Another option is to use a professional cleaning contractor. The key is to find a reputable company. To avoid con artists and unscrupulous fly-by-night operators, follow these guidelines:

- Require a copy of the contractor's general liability insurance certificate. Contact the insurer to make sure the policy is valid and current.

- Check with the local Better Business Bureau to verify that there is no history of complaints against the contractor.

- Ask for a minimum of three verifiable customer references. Contact each reference and ask how they were treated by the contractor and if they would hire him or her again. A reputable company will be eager to have the references checked because they know it means more business and more word-of-mouth advertising.

- Be sure to get written estimates.

- Make it a requirement that everyone involved in the clean up signs the state's version of a release of lien upon final payment.*

*In most states, any service provider who provides a service, labor, or materials for the improvement of real property has a right to file a lien against the property's title for nonpayment. In addition, the investor is still financially responsible if even he or she does pay a contractor for a job and he or she fails to pay the subcontractors who supplied the labor and the materials. If there is no legal proof that everyone involved was paid in full, the investor could end up holding the bag. Always have legal proof that everyone has been paid in full.

Finally, always do an inspection of the property before making final payment to a cleaning company to make sure all work has been completed satisfactorily. If there are discrepancies, make note of them and require that they be corrected.

Cost Worksheet for Property Cleanup				
Date	Cost of Materials	Cost of Labor	Other Items	Total Cost

16

QUALIFYING TENANTS

F ind the right tenants for the properties that are under lease option. That means qualifying them carefully. Applicants for residential properties might not have the strongest credit history since they most likely were not able to qualify for a conventional loan. Or, in some cases, they may be fearful of banks and lenders and are looking for a less complicated route to a home. It is important to carefully check their applications to make sure they meet the criteria for a qualified tenant. Following all federal housing/discrimination laws, check for items like:

- Gainful employment

- Household income

- Tenant history

- Possession of upfront money

Run a credit report to find out if they have debt and how large that debt is. Also find out why they have incurred debt. In some cases, the applicants may have run into unexpected medical expenses that have caused financial difficulties, but are otherwise sound applicants. In other cases, applicants may have bad credit card debt, foreclosures, landlord judgments, repossessions, etc. and these individuals will not make good tenants. In a bankruptcy situation, evaluate the situation carefully to see if the applicants are doing their best to recover and repay debt or if they have simply dug themselves into a hole through irresponsible actions. The former may end up being good tenants while the latter are obviously not good candidates for the property.

In general, find out why prospective tenants want the property and how respectfully they have treated previous landlords. If they are evasive about information or their past history, they are not good candidates. Avoid applicants who want the property in a hurry. First of all, candidates who have thought the process through carefully are desired because they make the best tenants. Second, anyone who wants the property quickly may well be running from a bad situation. Although circumstances will vary, the best bet is to look for applicants who have never owned a property. They tend to see a lease optioned property as their opportunity to achieve the American dream of owning their own home. That means they will tend to be responsible and willing to invest "sweat equity" to improve the property. They will possess the pride of a homeowner and not only generate income but also maintain and increase the value of your investment.

Throughout the entire application process, stick to the facts and obey all federal and state fair housing laws. Be sure to follow the guidelines as laid out in the federal Fair Housing Act as described as follows:

Title VIII of the Civil Rights Act of 1968

Thanks to the Fair Housing Act of 1968 (amended in 1974 and 1988), discrimination is no longer allowed in the realm of housing. It is illegal to discriminate against race, color, national origin, sex, family status, or disability. A person cannot refuse to sell or rent to any individual who is a member of one of those classes who makes a legitimate offer. Moreover, a landlord cannot even charge a higher security deposit or change the terms of a lease based on one's family status, i.e. the existence of children. It also illegal to ask for higher application fees based on race. It is also against the Fair Housing Act to lie to minorities and say there

Title VIII of the Civil Rights Act of 1968

are no units for sale or rent if it is untrue. Nor is it permissible for a real estate agent to steer a white person or family into a white neighborhood or a black person or family into a black neighborhood. Likewise, under the Fair Housing Act, a landlord must make reasonable accommodations for individuals with disabilities. If individuals feel they have suffered from discrimination based on race, sex, religion, family status, or national origin, they can file a lawsuit, in which case they must prove that the housing was available, they applied for it, they were rejected, and the house stayed on the market after they were rejected. If they can show that, a burden is then pushed upon the owner of the house to show a legitimate reason for denying them the house that is not based on their protected class.

Source: http://www.legal-definitions.com/real-estate-law/right-to-buy-a-home

Beyond the federal law, be knowledgeable about the local and state fair housing laws. They may extend beyond the requirements of Title VIII. For example, the city of Seattle prohibits discrimination in the following areas:

- Race

- Color

- Ancestry

- National origin

- Creed

- Religion

- Political ideology

- Age

- Marital status

- Sexual orientation

- Sensory, mental, or physical disabilities

- Parental status

- Participation in Section 8 program

Be prepared to adjust the application requirements somewhat depending on the market. If vacancy levels are high, it may be necessary to take a chance on applicants whom might be rejected in a low vacancy situation. Of course, anyone with a criminal record, questionable history, and a spotty employment record is likely not a good candidate. Sometimes, it is better to have a vacant property than to deal with the personal and legal hassle of coping with a bad tenant.

Perhaps the best way of qualifying tenants is to establish and write down personal guidelines for evaluating applicants. Use the same guidelines below as a reference to establish your own rules:

- No unpaid landlord tenant judgments

- Good references from previous landlords

- Gross monthly income equal to two (or three times) the monthly rental rate

If the decision is made to turn someone down, do it professionally and with compassion. After all, at some time in the future, they may come back as a potentially excellent tenant — all because they remembered the kindness with which they were treated.

17

MANAGING TENANTS — GOOD AND BAD

Once the lease option business is entered, an investor also becomes a property manager — and a manager of people. And that means dealing with all the good and bad traits of individuals. Let us look at good tenants first.

MANAGING GOOD TENANTS

Tenants are customers, and, as in any business, they should be treated well. It is not only the right thing to do; it also makes good business sense. After all, they are sources of the best kind of advertising — word-of-mouth. They will help spread an investor's reputation among their families, friends, and business associates. It does not have to be expensive to create and maintain good will with good tenants. As always, communication is the key. Send them birthday cards, holiday cards, etc. Phone them to make sure everything is going well in their lives and with the property. And, although they should have been made responsible for maintenance in the lease option contract, it never hurts to lend a helping hand; for example, mentioning good places to get bargains on paint, drapes, etc. This will help them save money while getting the benefit of an improved property. All in all, treat good tenants well and considerable rewards will be reaped in terms of good will, less hassle, and more word-of-mouth advertising.

MANAGING BAD TENANTS

In the lease option business, it is likely that a tenant who is late with payments, misses payments, does not maintain the property, or who disappears will be encountered. The best way to avoid this, of course, is to qualify applicants carefully upfront. It is proof of the old adage, "An ounce of prevention is worth a pound of cure." However, if a bad tenant slips through, then apply the steps described below.

Step 1: Try to work things out over the phone or in person.

Call or visit the tenant to pin down what the problem is. Sometimes, a tenant is experiencing financial difficulties through no fault of their own, has shown good faith in the past, and is committed to paying. In a case like this, consider accepting a partial payment and take the risk that they may not be able to pay. It is a matter of judgment. However, if excuses of "the dog ate my homework" variety start occurring, then this should set off some alarms. These are usually excuses similar to "My aunt/grandfather/ cousin died," "I lost my paycheck," "I did not get paid." In cases like this and when payments are consistently late or missed, it is obvious that the second step needs to be taken.

Step 2: Notify the tenant in writing of eviction.

If calls or visits did not rectify the situation, then it is time for eviction. This is a last resort, of course. Before this step, the investor should have stayed in reasonably close touch with the tenant so he or she has a feel for a reality of the situation. As mentioned above, some tenants are good people with unexpected problems. Others will flat out lie and have plenty of excuses.

No one likes to put individuals out of a home; however, it is paramount to remember that landlords have a duty to take care of themselves and their investors. Money is being lost when the tenant does not pay. Eviction is not an easy or pleasant process, but a landlord can safeguard himself or herself from the start by making sure the option contract has been worded so that it is subject to the rental agreement being followed. It can be wording similar to this: "This option will be declared null and void by the Optionor if any rental or option payment is made ten days or more late." The wording adds additional written legal underpinning for beginning the eviction process and provides the landlord with another layer of protection. To notify the tenant of eviction, be sure to send the letter via U.S. certified mail, return reply requested. In the letter, state clearly why the eviction proceedings have been instituted and attach a copy of the option agreement with the appropriate sections highlighted. Use wording similar to the letter below:

Dear _____,

Your rental payment is now 15 days overdue and this is a violation of the option agreement (attached). This is the fifth time you have been late. As a result, we are voiding the option agreement. Be advised that you have forfeited the right to buy this house.

Sincerely,
Name
Address

If legal steps needed to be taken to collect past due amounts, check with the state's regulations. They vary from state to state. For example, in some states, as a landlord, wages, bank accounts, state tax refunds, etc. can be garnished. In other states, the garnishment route cannot be taken. Another course to take is to employ the services of a collection agency, but their services are not cheap. They may take anywhere from 40 to 60 percent of the amount recovered.

An intermediate step before eviction is suggested by Matthew S. Chan in his book, *TurnKey Investing with Lease Options*. He recommends the "sign and leave" approach because he wants to avoid eviction whenever possible. It is a time consuming and costly step and, in his opinion, the last resort. He points out that up to 30–45 days of rental income can be lost from the time the eviction notice is filed until he gets legal possession of the property. In effect, Chan's "sign and leave" policy asks the tenant to relinquish legal possession of the property in exchange for not filing an eviction notice. It allows the tenant the opportunity to get out of the lease and leave peacefully. Chan then negotiates a settlement amount or lets the tenant go, depending on the amount owed. Be sure to check with a real estate attorney to see if this approach complies with the state's real property laws.

MORE DETAIL ON THE EVICTION PROCESS

Be sure to protect lease option investments in every way possible. It makes sense to acquire as much knowledge about evictions as possible — as unpleasant as the subject may be. Here are more details on the process so an investor can become knowledgeable on the subject and protect his or her lease option investments.

In legal terms, eviction is also known as *possession, unlawful detainer, forcible detainer,* or a *summary proceeding.* Basically, an eviction is a lawsuit to get a court order to remove a tenant. Remember, by law, a tenant cannot physically be removed from the premises. No matter how obnoxious the tenant has been, do not take steps like the following:

- Using or threatening to use force

- Interrupting or discontinuing essential services

- Removing the occupants' possessions from the dwelling

- Removing the entrance door

- Removing, plugging, or rendering inoperable the entrance door lock

- Changing the lock on the entrance door without supplying the occupant with a key

Before commencing with the proceeding, the tenancy must be terminated. This is done by serving notice on the tenant as required by the state law. The notice is typically three to five days for nonpayment of rent. After that time period, court proceedings can begin if the tenant has not paid the rent in full or moved out. The informal proceedings, much like a small claims court, can range from ten to 30 days.

Upon issuing a "judgment" or "order" in the landlord's favor, the court issues a legal document called a "warrant" or "writ". The warrant orders the appropriate enforcement agent to forcibly remove the tenant from the premises. The agent normally changes the locks and removes the personal property of the tenant. These days, few tenants are actually thrown out. Check with the county officials to see if the landlord is required to hire movers and store tenant property. Be sure to become familiar with landlord tenant laws in the county; however, it is not recommended to pursue evictions before a court on your own unless you are also an attorney. Hire an attorney to do the job. And, do not hire just any attorney; hire one who specializes in the area of landlord tenant law. To get practical advice at the ground level on dealing with evictions, talk to other experienced landlords in the city or town. They will be able to provide good hands on advice. If there is a landlord's association in the area, join it and gain access to the combined knowledge of its members.

Another method of dealing with evictions is advocated by attorney, entrepreneur and speaker, William Bronchick. He points out that evictions take time. In other words, the longer the defaulting tenant is in possession of the property, the more money can be lost. His strategy is to offer the tenant cash to leave right away. Although this may seem counter intuitive,

Bronchick points out that it makes good financial sense. He argues, if the matter can be settled quickly without going to court, do it. Of course, do not rely on the tenant's promise to move and pay him or her before they leave the property. Instead, wait until they vacate, clean the property, hand over the keys, and sign a written release of liability.

Bronchick also points out the need to deal with the security deposit, whether the tenant leaves voluntarily or by legal force. Security deposits are subject to state law whether or not a landlord is entitled to them. The rules are approximately the same in most states: the security deposit has to be returned within 30 days or a certified letter has to be sent to the tenant telling him or her of the reasons why it is being kept. Even if the landlord is entitled to retain the deposit, failure to follow the proper procedure will result in a lawsuit for improper withholding. Remember, the tenant can be sued in small claims court for rent owed and damages to the property; however, the landlord cannot withhold the security deposit without following the rules.

For additional information on eviction laws, read the overview provided at the end of this chapter.

HOW EVICTIONS WORK: RULES FOR LANDLORDS AND PROPERTY MANAGERS

An overview of the eviction process, including the termination notices required for different situations.

A landlord cannot begin an eviction lawsuit without first legally terminating the tenancy. This means giving the tenant adequate written notice, in a specified way and form. If the tenant does not move (or reform — for example, by paying the rent or finding a new home for the dog), a lawsuit to evict can then be filed. Technically, this is called an unlawful detainer, or UD, lawsuit. State laws set out very detailed requirements to end a tenancy. Different types of termination notices are required for different types of situations and each state has its own procedures as to how termination notices and eviction papers must be written and delivered.

Termination Notices

Although terminology varies somewhat from state to state, there are basically three types of termination notices for tenancies that landlords terminate due to tenant misbehavior:

- **Pay Rent or Quit Notices** are typically used when the tenant has not paid the rent. They give the tenant a few days (three to five in most states) to pay the rent or move out ("quit").

- **Cure or Quit Notices** are typically given after a tenant violates a term or condition of the lease or rental agreement, such as a "no pets" clause or the promise to refrain from making excessive noise. Usually, the tenant has a set amount of time in which to correct, or "cure," the violation. A tenant who fails to do so must move or face the possibility of an eviction lawsuit.

- **Unconditional Quit Notices** are the harshest of all. They order the tenant to vacate the premises with no chance to pay the rent or correct a lease or rental agreement violation. In most states, unconditional quit notices are allowed only when the tenant has:

    o Repeatedly violated a significant lease or rental agreement clause.

    o Been late with the rent on more than one occasion.

    o Seriously damaged the premises.

    o Engaged in serious illegal activity, such as drug dealing on the premises.

However, in some states, landlords may use **Unconditional Quit Notices** for transgressions that would require **Pay or Quit Notices** or **Cure or Quit Notices** in other, more tenant-friendly states. In these strict states, landlords may extend second chances if they wish, but no law requires them to do so. Landlords may use **30 Day** or **60 Day** to end a month-to-month tenancy when the tenant has not done anything wrong. Many rent control cities, however, go beyond state laws and require the landlord to prove a legally recognized reason for eviction ("just cause") of tenants. Following receipt of notice, if the tenant has not left or fixed the lease or rental agreement violation, the landlord must properly serve the tenant with a summons and complaint for eviction if the landlord still wants the tenant to leave.

Rationale for the Rules

Landlords often chafe at the detailed rules that they must follow. There is a reason, however, why most states have insisted on strict compliance. First of all, an eviction case is, relatively speaking, a very fast legal procedure. The price to pay for this streamlined treatment is unwavering adherence to the rules. Second, what is at stake here — a tenant's home — is arguably more important than a civil case concerning money or business. Consequently, legislators have been extra careful to see to it that the tenant gets adequate notice and an opportunity to respond.

Tenant Defenses

If the tenant decides to mount a defense, it may add weeks — even months — to the process. A tenant can point to mistakes in the notice or the eviction complaint or improper service of either in an attempt to delay or dismiss the case. The way that the landlord has conducted business with the tenant may also affect the outcome: If the rental unit is uninhabitable or the tenant thinks the landlord is retaliating, this may shift attention away from the tenant's wrongdoing and diminish the landlord's chances of victory.

Removal of the Tenant

If the landlord wins the unlawful detainer lawsuit, he or she will get a judgment for possession of the property and/or for unpaid rent. But the landlord cannot just move the tenant and his things out onto the sidewalk — trying to remove a tenant can cause a lot of trouble.

Be Careful Removing Tenants' Abandoned Property

A few states allow landlords to freely dispose of property a tenant leaves behind after moving out. Even in these states, this is legal only if it is quite clear that the tenant has left permanently, intending to turn the place over to the owner. In many states, landlords must follow storage and notification procedures.

Typically, a landlord must give the court judgment to a local law enforcement officer along with a fee that the tenant has paid as part of the costs to bring suit. The sheriff or marshal gives the tenant a notice that the officer will be back within a number of days to physically remove the tenant if he is not gone by then.

For More Help

Unless a landlord thoroughly knows his or her legal rights and duties before evicting a tenant, and unless every "i" is dotted and every "t" is crossed the landlord may end up on the losing side. For help preparing and serving termination notices and the eviction summons and complaint, see one of the following guides by Nolo:

Every Landlord's Legal Guide (National), by Marcia Stewart and attorneys Ralph Warner and Janet Portman.

The California Landlord's Law Book: Evictions, by attorney David Brown.

The New York Landlord's Law Book, by attorney Mary Ann Hallenborg.

18

RESELLING LEASE OPTIONS — MAKING YOUR PROFIT

The objective in buying lease options is to make a profit by gaining control of undervalued properties, but that profit is not made until the option is resold. The key to resale is marketing the property to a targeted audience. For example, assume a small commercial property that is in a perfect spot for a restaurant has been gained. The area in which it is located is in the path of progress and several office buildings have been built and occupied, and others are in the process of being built. The investor has done the research and found that the area lacks cafés and restaurants. Customers who are involved in the hospitality trade are the target market. To find prospective buyers, the investor goes online and runs a search for restaurant associations, franchises, etc. He or she checks with the local Chamber of Commerce to uncover potential customers, etc. Then, using this information, he or she draws up a list of the most likely buyers and contacts them. Local buyers can be contacted personally and provided with the property information. Using e-mail, distant prospects can be reached by sending them a property fact sheet and a photo of the property. Using this approach, the investor likely to resell the option for a profit within a few months because an attractive area was targeted and customers were targeted instead of marketing to anyone and everyone.

To resell a lease option for a profit, its value has to be calculated first. The price has to be as attractive to the buyer as the property itself. The objective is not to get greedy, but to create a win-win situation so everyone walks away from the deal happy. Circumstances vary, but here is an example of a win-win scenario. Assume a person has a property under control that has a fair market value of $350,000. This person has an option to buy it for $290,000. The general rule is to sell the option for ten percent of the property's market value. This would be $35,000. But do not forget that a person wants to be compensated for the time and effort spent in getting control of the property in the first place. Assume a person put $5,000 worth of time and effort into the deal. Add that $5,000 to $35,000 to get a $40,000 sales price. This allows the buyer of the option to get control of the property for $20,000 below market value. The result — win-win. To calculate the cost of the time and effort that has been put into the obtaining of a lease option, take into consideration the following factors: property search costs, real estate option purchase costs, maximizing appeal costs, marketing costs, and time spent on the entire process.

PROPERTY PACKAGING — SELLING THE SIZZLE AND THE STEAK

How much an investor is able to resell an option for is directly related to how well the property is marketed. And that brings us back to a subject we covered earlier in the book — benefits. Prospective buyers of the lease option need to clearly see how the purchase of that option will benefit them; otherwise, there will not be interest in the property, and the investor will not make the profit he or she deserves. It is vital that an investor not only targets the appropriate prospective buyers, but markets effectively to those buyers. This is particularly true of commercial/industrial properties. Unlike residential properties, they do not have the built in personal appeal of a home where a family will live. Commercial/industrial properties may have several different uses and customers need to see what uses these buildings can be put to. For example, one building/property might serve as an auto repair shop, a drug store, a gift shop, a coffee shop, etc, but potential buyers of the lease option may not see these possibilities if the vision is not created for them. One way of creating that vision is through property information sheets, much like the ones seen in the boxes outside residential properties. Of course, the sheet should have a good photo of the building/property. The text of the sheet should describe the physical structure of the building in terms of benefits; e.g., "modern building built in 1995 with light, airy space, and fully up-to-date HVAC (heating, ventilation, air conditioning) for low energy costs and easy maintenance." The description should also include the geographical area and tout its benefits as well; e.g., "centrally located in the heart of booming downtown area with easy access to transportation, lots of customer traffic," etc. Describe the interior as well so potential option buyers can get an idea of the dimensions and shape of the space to see if they will meet the specific needs of their business. All in all, the property information sheet should provide a compact and inviting description of the building. It will help one's mind set to think of the sheet not as a property description per se, but as a sales document — a one page sales brochure designed to lure buyers into contacting the investor about a great opportunity. And, remember, the property information sheet does not have to be only in print. Make use of many other marketing techniques to get the word out. We will look at those next.

The Internet

The great advantage of the Internet is that a person is no longer restricted to marketing locally, regionally, or nationally. An added advantage is that, at the present time, foreign investors love American real estate and actively seek it out because of the stability of our country and, of course, the great profit potential. Another advantage is that many foreign investors are cash buyers, which allows an investor to avoid the hassle of dealing with lenders and mortgage brokers. Tap into global market in three ways:

- **Web pages** — This should be a properties for sale Web site that is easily accessible by viewers. Avoid fancy graphics that slow downloads and cause customers to get impatient and move on to another site. The pages should include photographs of the property, its location, directions to the property, the site plan, features, the sale price, terms, appointment information, etc. Maps can be found at online mapping services like:

    o Expedia — **http://www.google.com/**

    o Google — **http://maps.google.com/**

    o MapQuest — **http://maps.google.com/**

    o Yahoo — **http://maps.yahoo.com/**

- **Online ads** — There are many Web sites on which properties can be advertised. Here is a sampling of sites:

    o Apartments for Sale — **http://apartmentsforsale.com/**

    o ApartmentSales — **http://apartmentsales.com/**

    o BizTrader — **http://biztrader.com/**

    o LoopNet — **http://www.loopnet.com**

    o Realtyinvestor.com — **http://realtyinvestor.com/**

    o ReBuz — **http://rebuz.com/**

- **URL forwarding** — Use this inexpensive service on the web page. It allows the property for sale domain name to be forwarded to a specific web page on the Web site. It eliminates the necessity of having to build an entirely new Web site for the property sale domain name.

Traditional Marketing/Advertising Tools

Do not make the mistake of relying solely on the Internet to market lease optioned properties. The noise in today's business market is so great that the only way to cut through the clutter is to have a complete marketing mix. Include traditional methods like the following:

- **For Sale Signs** — Always have a professional sign placed in a highly visible spot on the property. The lettering should be highly readable so passers-by can comprehend the message quickly and easily. The signs should be durable, waterproof, and contain the Web site address, e-mail address, and telephone number. A typical sign might look like this:

> **Property for Sale**
> **www.jonesproperties.com**
> **Sales@jonesproperties.com**
> **Call (xxx) xxx-xxxx now!**

- **Classified Ads** — Place ads in the local daily and weekly newspapers with the same information as above. Also, many newspapers now have online classified ads so be sure to place ads on these sites as well.

SELLING THE LEASE OPTION

Once a buyer has been found, then it is time to transfer the ownership of the option. This is done through an *assignment of real estate option* agreement. The lease option holder is the *assignor* and the buyer is the *assignee* and both sign an agreement. Be sure the agreement is signed in the presence of a notary public.

Once the agreement has been signed, the Optioner of the assignment must be notified. Do this by sending a Notice of Assignment by U.S. Postal Service Certified Mail. Be sure a return receipt is requested so there is proof that the notification was received. And do not forget to send a copy to the attorney or escrow or title agent holding the property title documents in escrow. A sample notification is shown below:

July 12, 2007

Thomas T. Barnes
(Address)
(City, State, ZIP)

Dear Mr. Barnes

Be advised that on this twelfth day of July, 2007, I have assigned all my rights and interest in the Real Estate Option Agreement, executed by you as Optioner, to me, as Optionee, on (date) to Samuel P. Smith, whose post office mailing address is (city, state, ZIP).

A copy of the Assignment of Real Estate Option Agreement is attached to this letter of notification.

Sincerely,

John K. Jones

TAX CONSIDERATIONS

Income earned from real estate option sales is taxed at the same rate as ordinary earned income. For tax purposes, the Internal Revenue Service considers an investor to be a real estate dealer and not an investor because he or she is buying options with the intent to resell and not as an investment. Section 1234 of the Internal Revenue Code covers real estate options. The rules are shown below. For complete information and updates, go to **http://www.irs.gov/**. This information can be difficult to find and read on the IRS site; it may be easier to simply do a search for Section 1234. Of course, tax regulations can be horrendously complicated so our recommendation is to find a tax professional to handle these matters. He or she should be licensed to represent the investor before all administrative levels of the IRS. Avoid using off-the-shelf tax programs for the simple reason that they cannot represent a person in front of the IRS. A well qualified tax professional will keep an investor from having to appear in the first place, so, all in all, the fee for his or her services is money well spent.

Sec. 1234. Options to Buy or Sell

a) Treatment of gain or loss in the case of the purchaser

   (1) General rule

      Gain or loss attributable to the sale or exchange of, or loss attributable to failure to exercise, an option to buy or sell property shall be considered gain or loss from the sale or exchange of property which has the same character as the property to which the option relates has in the hands of the taxpayer (or would have in the hands of the taxpayer if acquired by him).

   (2) Special rule for loss attributable to failure to exercise option

      For purposes of paragraph (1), if loss is attributable to failure to exercise an option, the option shall be deemed to have been sold or exchanged on the day it expired.

   (3) Nonapplication of subsection

      This subsection shall not apply to —

        (A) an option which constitutes property described in paragraph (1) of section 1221(a);

Sec. 1234. Options to Buy or Sell

(B) in the case of gain attributable to the sale or exchange of an option, any income derived in connection with such option which, without regard to this subsection, is treated as other than gain from the sale or exchange of a capital asset; and

(C) a loss attributable to failure to exercise an option described in section 1233(c).

(b) Treatment of grantor of option in the case of stock, securities, or commodities

(1) General rule

In the case of the grantor of the option, gain or loss from any closing transaction with respect to, and gain on lapse of, an option in property shall be treated as a gain or loss from the sale or exchange of a capital asset held not more than one year.

(2) Definitions

For purposes of this subsection —

(A) Closing transaction

The term "closing transaction" means any termination of the taxpayer's obligation under an option in property other than through the exercise or lapse of the option.

B) Property

The term "property" means stocks and securities (including stocks and securities dealt with on a "when issued" basis), commodities, and commodity futures.

Sec. 1234. Options to Buy or Sell

(3) Nonapplication of subsection

This subsection shall not apply to any option granted in the ordinary course of the taxpayer's trade or business of granting options.

(c) Treatment of options on section 1256 contracts and cash settlement options

(1) Section 1256 contracts

Gain or loss shall be recognized on the exercise of an option on a section 1256 contract (within the meaning of section 1256(b).

(2) Treatment of cash settlement options

(A) In general

For purposes of subsections (a) and (b), a cash settlement option shall be treated as an option to buy or sell property.

(B) Cash settlement option

For purposes of subparagraph (A), the term "cash settlement option" means any option which on exercise settles in (or could be settled in) cash or property other than the underlying property.

19

EXERCISING YOUR OPTION

In the course of business, an investor will eventually come across and acquire an option on a property he or she really wants to keep. As with the other transactions described earlier in the book, be sure to have a real estate attorney be involved in the closing of an exercise of option. This is no time for a mistake or an overlooked detail.

The first step in exercising a real estate option is to notify the optionor by sending him or her a Notice of Exercise of Real Estate Option letter like the sample below:

February 6, 2007

Ms. Jennifer Smith
(Address, City, ZIP)
Ms. Smith,

I am writing to notify you that as of the date above, I have chosen to exercise the real estate option given by you to me on October 10, 2006 to purchase the property therein described, pursuant to the terms and conditions of our Real Estate Option Agreement and Real Estate Purchase Agreement held in escrow by Mr. William Jones Attorney-at-Law, whose law office is located at 1234 Main St., Anytown, (state, ZIP).

Sincerely,
Thomas Toms

Send the letter by U.S. Postal Service Certified Mail and request a return receipt. This way there is verifiable proof that the document was received by the optionor. And do not forget to send a copy of the notification letter to the attorney or escrow/title agent holding all of the property title transfer documents in escrow.

Once the option has been exercised, the lease option holder has to buy the property under option or assign the agreement to a third party. In escrow, a purchase agreement should already be signed by the optionor. Plus, the purchase agreement should have been included as an addendum to the option agreement. If not, be sure to include a clause in the agreement stating that it would automatically turn into a purchase agreement once the option was exercised. Be sure to have worked out exactly how the property sale would be handled once the option is exercised.

Do not use the generic real estate purchase agreements used by real estate licensees in the state to record the purchase of a property under option. They are written not to protect the buyer, but the licensees' commissions and the legal rights and interests of the sellers who have listed their property through real estate brokers. Be sure to hire a real estate attorney who will draft a document that protects the rights and interests of the buyer. The items on the next page should be included in the document.

It is also important for the buyer to protect himself or herself in the case of unexpected problems that can occur during closing. That is why contingency clauses need to be included in the agreement. Here are three that should definitely be included:

- Approval of the property's title status and marketability — The buyer must approve these items before the transaction is closed. This is a protection in the case that liens or lawsuits have been filed against the property's title or owner since the option was purchased. Liens or lawsuits can adversely affect the marketability of the property.

- Approval of the property's existing loans — This needs to be done before the transaction is closed. It provides protection in the event that any of the property's loans are in foreclosure.

- Vacation of the property and grounds — Before the transaction is closed, the seller must be out of the property and the grounds. This protects the buyer from hostile property owners or tenants who refuse to leave after the sale is closed.

A sample purchase agreement was included earlier in the book so the buyer can familiarize himself or herself with the general stipulations. Remember, however, to always use an attorney to draw up an agreement that meets all of the state's real estate standards.

KEY STIPULATIONS

- **Assignment of the purchase agreement:** Stipulate the right to assign or sell the purchase agreement to a third party.

- **Default by buyer:** Stipulate that the earnest money paid is the sole remedy in the event that the buyer or buyer's assigns fail to close on the purchase of the property.

- **Default seller:** Stipulate that the buyer or buyer's assigns will have the right of specific performance in the event the seller defaults on the agreement by refusing to sell the property.

- **Description of property:** The agreement should include an exact legal description that is written on the recorded deed of the property in the purchase agreement.

- **Earnest money deposit:** Stipulate that the option fee is to be used as the earnest money deposit and applied toward the down payment.

- **Eminent domain action:** Stipulate that the buyer or buyer's assigns will be entitled to a full refund of the earnest money deposit paid, plus any accrued interest, if the property is condemned by eminent domain prior to the closing date.

KEY STIPULATIONS

• **Entry right:** Stipulate that the buyer or the buyer's assigns have the right to enter the property and inspect, repair, market, and show it to third parties prior to the closing date. At least 24 hours' notice must be given to the owner.

• **Examination of records:** Stipulate that the buyer or buyer's assignments have the right to examine all financial and tax records associated with the property prior to the closing date.

• **Marketable title:** Stipulate that the buyer must be capable of obtaining an owner's title insurance policy commitment letter from a title insurer in order to close on the purchase of the property.

• **Parties to the agreement:** Be specific and designate all parties to the purchase agreement as buyer and seller. This should include their legal status as to whether they are a single individual, husband and wife, or a business entity.

• **Purchase price:** Stipulate that the firm purchase price of the property is the same as the purchase price listed in the option agreement.

• **Refund of option fee in case of damage or destruction:** Stipulate a full refund of the earnest money deposit paid, plus accrued interest, if the property incurs damage or destruction from earthquakes, fires, thunderstorms, etc. prior to the closing date.

• **Terms of purchase:** Stipulate exactly how the property purchase is going to be financed.

• **Vacation of property:** Stipulate that the seller must completely vacate the property and grounds prior to the closing date.

THE REAL ESTATE SETTLEMENT PROCEDURES ACT (RESPA)

This statute was enacted in 1974 to protect the property-buying public from being cheated by the real estate industry. Part of the RESPA statement reads:

> *The Congress finds that significant reforms in the real estate settlement process are needed to insure that consumers throughout the Nation are provided with greater and more timely information on the nature and costs of the settlement process and are protected from unnecessarily high settlement charges caused by certain abusive practices that have developed in some areas of the country...*

The real estate industry is defined as:

- Attorneys (performing real estate settlements or closings)

- Escrow companies

- Mortgage and deed of trust lenders

- Mortgage brokers

- Real estate agents

The agency responsible for enforcing the statute nationwide is the Department of Housing and Urban Development (HUD). According to the Web site, the objectives of RESPA are:

> *RESPA* is about closing costs and settlement procedures. *RESPA* requires that consumers receive disclosures at various times in the transaction and outlaws kickbacks that increase the cost of settlement services. *RESPA* is a *HUD* consumer protection statute designed to help home buyers be better shoppers in the home buying process, and is enforced by *HUD*.

To find out more about RESPA, can log onto the HUD page at (**http:// www.hud.gov/offices/hsg/sfh/res/respa_hm.cfm**).

ADDITIONAL TASKS

Once the closing has been scheduled, there are certain essential tasks that still must be completed. First, have all the utility meters read on the day before closing. This is particularly important with commercial/industrial properties where utility costs can run high. Have the appropriate utility company read the meters so the buyer does not get billed for services that are the responsibility of the previous owner.

Second, stipulate that the 365 day method is to be used to prorate the property taxes. This item cannot be calculated and included on the HUD 1 Settlement Statement at the time it is signed by the optionor and the optionee. Until the actual sale date is known, property tax prorations can be calculated. As the name indicates, the method is based on the premise that every year has 365 days. For example, if the annual property tax bill for a rental property is $5,300 and the seller owned the property for 250 days, the seller's prorated tax portion would be $3,630 ($5,300 ÷ 365 = $14.52 x 250). If, for some reason, the current year's property taxes cannot be determined, state in the closing statement that any estimated tax proration will be readjusted on receipt of the tax bill.

Third, if the closing is on a rental property, try to close the transaction on the last day of the month. This means that the buyer will be in possession of the property on the first day of the month which is the day on which rental payments are usually due. The buyer will also be able to collect rental payments and initiate eviction proceedings against any tenants who do not pay. In addition, rental payments will not need to be prorated.

Finally, be sure to do a walk-through on the property on the day of the closing. Bring along a still or video camera and record everything. Check for such problems as standing water, termites, rodents, environmental hazards, and condemnation/code violation notices posted on the property. This is an important duty to perform in case there are any problems the owner has hidden from the buyer or neglected to mention. Use a checklist as part of the walk through to make sure nothing is missed. Also, use it to check and double check the loan, transfer, and closing documents. Once the agreement is signed, it is very difficult to correct mistakes.

Be sure to review the following areas:

- Title insurance policy for exceptions

- Property survey

- Hazard insurance policy

- Termite/pest control inspection report

- Bill of sale for personal property

- Deed

- Promissory note

- Mortgage or deed of trust loan documents

- Loan assumption documents

- HUD I settlement statement*

Also, check with governmental agencies on these areas:

- Building, fire, health, and safety violations

- Environmental hazards citations

- Municipal liens

And verify the following areas:

- Legal descriptions of the property

- Zoning designations of the property

- Property tax payment status

- Issuance of current certificate of occupancy for the property

*HUD allows the buyer and the seller to review the HUD 1 Settlement Statement 24 hours in advance of the scheduled closing date. Be sure to review it to make sure everything is correct and no unknown fees have been included. PDF files of the statement are easily available on the Internet at HUD and many other sites.

20

BUSINESS ADMINISTRATION

Only simple administrative tools and organization will be needed when first starting out in the lease options business. However, it is an absolute necessity to be highly organized and professional as the business grows. Records will grow more complex along with tax considerations and disorganization can cost money, tenants, and, possibly, trouble with the Internal Revenue Service. Right from the start, put an efficient and effective system into place to keep all real estate dealings straight and easy to manage. In this chapter, we have provided guidelines to aid in the achievement of that objective.

GUIDELINE 1: LIVE IN THE COMPUTER AGE

Computers and computer applications are one of the greatest boons to today's business person because they relieve us of so many tedious tasks and make them easier to accomplish which, in turn, frees us to concentrate on more important things. A modest investment in the following areas can reap great dividends for a person in all aspects of the lease option business.

First, get a high-speed Internet connection. It could be either direct subscriber link (DSL) or cable. Avoid dial-up connections. They are far too slow for business needs, tie up phone lines, and cause frustration. With a high-speed connection, a person can easily access and update a Web site, as well as send property photos, letters, large files, etc. Also, the capability of expanding the connection to handle several users with the use of a router is possible. Essentially, a router gives a person an inexpensive way to expand the business and communication efforts.

Second, install a local area network if an office with several computers is being used. It allows the business to operate more efficiently in terms of information and file sharing. All that is needed is another router and cables to connect the computers to each other. Major computer companies like Microsoft have applications that can be easily installed and configured once all the necessary hardware and connections are in place.

Third, if the business expands and acquires many properties, property management software will be needed. As the name suggests, these applications specialize in leases, rental properties, reporting, tenants, utilities, etc. and will make life much easier.

Fourth, buy a general business accounting/bookkeeping application to handle financial statements and reporting. Check with tax specialists on the team to see which ones they recommend. That will make sure the systems are coordinated. Well known applications include Oracle, QuickBooks, Peachtree Accounting, and MYOB Accounting.

GUIDELINE 2: ORGANIZE YOUR PAPERWORK

Paperwork is still a substantial part of the real estate system — contracts, documents, receipts, statements, etc. — and all these items need to be kept straight and easy to access. Color coding folders can provide quick recognition of categories. For example, have one yellow coded folder for lease option sellers and one blue coded folder for lease option buyers. The seller folder would contain such items as:

- Contracts

- Mortgage documents

- Subject-to documents

- Correspondence

- Surveys

- Inspections

- Photos

The buyer folder would contain such items as:

- Applications

- Credit reports

- Payment copies

- Bills

- Maintenance records

- Property photos

- Digital film of property

With any folder, document everything possible — tenant calls, maintenance efforts, etc. This information can come in handy if a tenant or other person decides to sue for something like a supposed accident on the property. Documentation will be available to prove their case wrong. Think of documentation as an insurance policy against the unforeseen and keep the records far beyond the time a particular property is sold.

In general, keep track of everything and keep it up-to-date and readily at hand. Nothing can be more frustrating than being unable to find a document when it is really needed.

GUIDELINE 3: AS YOU GROW, DELEGATE

When a business becomes so complex and time consuming that it takes time from the main objective — making a profit — then it is time to consider hiring an office manager, secretary, receptionist, etc. Remember the main purpose is to generate business and profits; the investor should not be concentrating on minor tasks that take away from that purpose. Every successful entrepreneur knows the truth of this statement and learns how to delegate non-essential tasks to a person better qualified to handle these duties. As a business grows, delegation will be a crucial factor in success. Beyond increasing effectiveness, it also offers the following benefits:

- **Reduced stress** — Sometimes entrepreneurs tend to think they need to do everything themselves or it will not get done right. This is a mistake designed to inflate the ego and is a recipe for burnout. Worse, it makes a person lose sight of the big picture and focus on unimportant details. Delegation allows a person to stay sharp and concentrate on important goals and objectives. At the same time, it helps with relaxation and confidence.

- **Team development** — Once an office manager or other employees are added, they should function as a team and all pull in the same direction. That makes for a smooth, effective, and efficient organization. But team development should go beyond that. By delegating responsibilities, full potential of the team can be delegated and they can contribute their ideas and creativity to the business.

- **Multiplication of effectiveness** — When team members know that their ideas, opinions, and efforts are valued, a person, in effect, is multiplying himself or herself. That is because they recognize the investor's commitment to them and that, in turn, spurs their commitment in terms of making the business even more successful.

- **Increased business presence in the market** — A high-functioning team tells tenants, sellers, buyers, and the real estate market at large that a high standard of professionalism and effectiveness is maintained. That means they will want to do more business with the business because they know that not only will the entire team treat them fairly but it will reduce risk and increase income and profitability. Put simply, the market will judge a business by the actions of its team members so why not make sure all members act to the highest standards of professionalism?

Some business people are reluctant to delegate because they feel it takes too much time and effort. This misses the point of delegation altogether. Time spent training up front actually saves time and money in the long run. That is because, when employees are trained right at the beginning, then their mistakes and behavior will not need to be corrected later on. Also, keep in mind that delegation does not have to be complicated. Here are the keys to delegation.

First, look for gaps in one's own skills, knowledge, and abilities and look for a person who can fill those gaps. For example, if a person knows he or she is not good at organizing files, then it makes sense to hire an office manager to handle these duties.

Second, select the right person for the job. In the case of an office manager, a person with the appropriate training and years of experience in the position would be ideal. Or, if a person who's new to the position needs to be hired, provide them with the training they require to carry out their tasks. It can be as simple as sitting down with them and showing them what needs to be done or as complex as having them attend a seminar, workshop, or college course.

Third, communicate very clearly to team members what they should accomplish in their positions. This is an often overlooked aspect of delegation. Some employers think they should throw an employee into a position and let them sink or swim. This is the wrong attitude. Remember, the business and its reputation is at stake, so letting a new employee flounder around and possibly making mistakes could cost money or customers. Another negative is that this approach does not contribute to team cohesiveness. It creates an "every man for himself" attitude and destroys team spirit. Be very clear on the results desired from employees and then judge them on the accomplishment of those results.

Fourth, set time frames for the accomplishment of employee tasks. Nothing can create more confusion than a vague, "Get this done, will you?" To one person, this phrase may mean, "Get it done by Friday." But an employee cannot read minds and, since time is different for everyone, he or she might interpret the request as, "Well, it does not look important, so I will put it at the bottom of the pile while I work on more important items." This can lead to unpleasant consequences, like when a contract does not go out on time and ends up costing the business a lucrative deal. Be specific and clear and say something similar to, "This contract needs to be completed and mailed by January 31."

Fifth, treat team members with respect. For example, do not order them about. Instead, request that they take on jobs and let them know that their efforts and ideas are appreciated. Offer them honest praise for jobs well done. This is not only important for the employee's personal satisfaction; it also demonstrates to everyone on the team that delegation delivers rewards beyond just doing the job. The effect will be that they will want to work much harder. Treating team members with respect not only make good personal sense; it also makes good business sense.

Sixth, when delegating, really delegate. Do not stand over their shoulders and monitor everything they do. It is annoying and counter-productive. It makes people nervous and when they get nervous, they make mistakes.

Seventh, immediately after training people in their jobs, follow up with them. They are sure to have questions and those questions need to be answered. Explain upfront that their progress will be monitored and offer any additional assistance if it is needed. Establish the expectation that questions from them are actively encouraged. Some employees are afraid to ask questions because they see it as a sign of weakness. Establishing the expectation will let them know that questions are okay. A new team member will most likely require more monitoring while an experienced team member will require less.

It is likely that the first team member hired will be an office manager or property manager. Beyond experience, we recommend that these fundamental traits and skills are looked for in such an employee:

- **Computer skilled** — Nobody gets by in business these days without computer skills, so the person hired should be literate in such areas as word processing skills, spreadsheets, letter writing, etc. If the person in mind does not possess those skills, then provide training.

- **Detail-oriented** — Since he or she will be tracking correspondence, late fees, option fees, tenant's rent, utility bills, etc., they will need to document all this information in detailed form.

- **Firm** — It is a fact of real estate life that there will be some tenants who try to pay late or make unreasonable demands. A good office or property manager will not be a pushover for these irresponsible individuals. He or she will stand firm and expect payment on time.

- **Follow-through** — An office manager or property manager needs to stay on top of and take care of the details that could cost money — follow up on heating and air conditioning in vacant properties (has it been turned on or off?), confirmation of delivery of documents (contracts, etc.), and the dozens of other items that go along with properties.

- **Independence and initiative** — A self-starter as an office manager or property manager is desired. After all, it is likely that the investor will be out and about visiting properties, meeting with buyers and sellers, etc., so someone has to hold down the fort. They should be able to make independent judgments that will contribute to the profitability of the operation.

- **Organization** — Organization is a key skill in the business of lease options and all other areas of real estate. A great office or property manager will have everything at hand and be able to retrieve it at a moment's notice. There are times when things will need to move quickly to seal a deal or resolve a problem.

- **Even-tempered and pleasant** — With the territory of lease options and other areas of real estate comes the fact that a person will be dealing with some unhappy people. An even-tempered manager who does not lose his or her cool can calm down an irate tenant or prevent the investor from making rash statements.

21

THINKING STRATEGICALLY

As an investor grows more successful in the lease options business, he or she may want to expand efforts in that area and other areas of real estate as well. If that course is chosen, then realize one important point — real estate investment is decidedly not an individual endeavor. It requires teamwork and the investor needs to be the leader of that team. As additional fields of real estate are moved into, it will be found that much more knowledge is required in the areas of mortgages, financing, markets, taxes, etc. Take the time to master as much of this knowledge as possible, but mastery of all knowledge is not the investor's role. It is the investor's job to find profitable properties and investments and use the expertise of the team to achieve that objective. But the team will also be a synergy machine. That is, by building the team, a network of contacts and influence is constructed. That network then generates leads which, in turn, produce more opportunities. A team also allows an investor to stay on top of the market and grab opportunities fast before the competition finds them. Members of a team will vary. Along with real estate attorneys and property appraisers, here are some others to consider adding to the team:

- Contractors/repairmen

- Financial consultant

- Lenders/mortgage brokers

- Real estate brokers or agents

- Tax advisors

Add members to the team as befits the situation. Keep in mind that each of these individuals has a specialty, and it is their expertise that should be tapped into in order to evaluate, acquire, and maintain/improve properties. Mortgages are the province of the lender. The tax advisor provides advice on legal issues regarding federal, state, and local tax laws. The appraiser evaluates properties and lets an investor know if they are worthwhile. In effect, each of these team members is a source of valuable information and they provide two important benefits. One, they prevent the investor from wasting his or her time and money on unsuitable properties. And, two, they increase the bottom line. It is important to assemble a great team and to treat each member in a great fashion. Keep in mind that it is a two-way street. In return for providing benefits, team members should receive referrals and good word-of-mouth from an investor. Also, remember that the building of a team is not done overnight. An investor has to gain trust from others regarding honesty, business sense, etc., and, in turn, they have to be trusted. Ideally, people for the team who are highly regarded in the real estate community and the general community will be found.

If a person is new to lease options or other aspects of the real estate market, the best way to build a reputation as a professional — and a team — is to go out and complete successful deals. The proof is in the pudding, as far as other real estate professionals are concerned. They do not have time for fools and incompetents — there is too much money at stake. They want to see evidence that a person has every day business sense combined with a creative flair for doing deals. Once that evidence is provided by working successfully with other professionals, then it is time to start building a network team. The key to this is regular communication. It does not have to be anything fancy like a meeting. Sometimes the best deals are done over a casual cup of coffee or at lunch. Underlying all communication should be the rock solid fact that an investor always keeps his or her word from the simplest appointment to the most complex meeting.

Now, let us look at some of members that need to be part of the team and their role in creating a person's success as an investor.

THE TAX ADVISOR

Tax advantages are one of the great benefits of real estate investment. Naturally, a person has to know what those benefits are before in order to take advantage of them. A tax advisor can help out greatly in not only this area, but in the area of tax law. The Internal Revenue Service tax regulations are complex and, often, impossible to decipher. That is where tax advisors come in. Their specialty is the knowledge of IRS rules and regulations and they make sure the investor stays in compliance with them. Moreover, they can help shape and refine investment goals and form an overall investment strategy.

The chosen advisor should specialize in real estate investing or at least have considerable experience in the field. As with other team members, check the references and reputations of local tax advisors. To get a good sense of their expertise and communication skills, interview them. During the interview, they should demonstrate a good understanding of the investment objectives and provide specific ideas on how to achieve those objectives. For example, an investor is looking for quick cash from properties, the tax advisor should provide specific knowledge on how to minimize tax liabilities and maximize the investment. On the other hand, if an investor is looking to build wealth over time, that same advisor should offer long-term strategies to achieve growth and income for a secure future. Look also for a tax advisor who is able to steer the investor toward specific types of properties that will help achieve goals. In addition, they should also be able to recommend specific types of ownership (direct or indirect ownership, etc.).

THE LENDER OR MORTGAGE BROKER

In real estate investments in and beyond lease options, it is likely that an investor will need to borrow money and that means gaining knowledge of available loans. Although there are many sources, the two main ones to tap into are the lender and mortgage broker. Both are in the business of giving customers cash and charging rent for it; in other words, they make money by offering loans. The differences between the two are the ways in which they operate.

Lenders

A lender is any public or private firm that directly loans a person the money needed to buy a property. They are often called direct lenders. Within this category, banks, credit unions, and private lenders are found. Some lenders offer loans in a variety of areas while others may specialize in specific types of loans.

Mortgage Brokers

Mortgage brokers are considered indirect lenders. Their role in life is to present a loan request to a number of different lenders in order to find the best financing. In other words, they broker deals by acting as intermediaries.

Neither lenders nor mortgage brokers are objective and that should be kept in mind. Their objective is to find the maximum amount of money a person can borrow, not necessarily the amount he or she can afford. It will pay for an investor to work with them in an equally objective manner. It is also important to remember that lenders and brokers operate on the premise of minimization of risk; in other words, they want to know, with reasonable assurance, that they will get their money back with interest. They want and need to make a profit. And, in the case of banks and credit unions, the lenders are using the money of depositors and, therefore, tend to be conservative in the loans they make. As discussed earlier in the book, that means they look closely at a person's credit rating before making a loan. They also cast an eagle eye on collateral. Collateral is real or personal property that a person pledges to secure the loan or mortgage. If a person fails to pay the debt, then the lender has the right to take the collateral and sell it to recover the outstanding principle and interest on the loan. In the case of real estate, the purchased property is usually the pledged collateral for real estate loans or mortgages.

Since lenders or mortgage brokers are important sources of funds for real estate endeavors, it is vital to build solid relationships with them. The first step in that process is to identify and seek out lenders who specialize in the type of properties being targeted. The second step is to meet with them and give them the latest personal financial statement. Be upfront about one's financial position right from the start. Exaggerating the truth about a financial situation is the quickest way to break trust and trust is the one asset that needs to be established from the beginning. Also, lender/brokers require supporting documents about income and assets and they will do a credit check to verify a person's status. These tight controls are a result of the early 1990s saving and loans scandals and are designed to prevent abuse of the system. Before meeting with a lender or broker, be sure to be prepared to meet all requirements for verification.

The best choices are experienced lenders or brokers who fully understand the local real estate market and its fluctuations. As a result of their experience, they can be objective and can prevent an investor from making bad mistakes.

Lenders/brokers are inherently conservative and that can be an extremely important quality in times of wildly inflated prices that have no basis in reality. Their cautious approach can prevent an investor from losing a lot of money.

THE REAL ESTATE BROKER AND AGENT

We addressed the subject of brokers and agents earlier in the book, but only from the standpoint of lease options. If an investor decides to expand into areas other than lease options, then he or she will definitely need the best and most experienced brokers and agents as part of the team. Here is a brief refresher on the difference between a broker and an agent. A real estate broker is the highest level of state licensed professional. The broker supervises licensed real estate agents who are qualified to handle real estate listings and transactions. Unless an investor is involved in large, complicated transactions, he or she will be dealing with real estate agents most of the time. But, whichever one is being dealt with, verify that the person has a good and solid track record with investment property transactions in the area being targeted. Also, when working with a real estate agent, know what kind of agency he or she represents. It can make a difference in one's profits. Generally speaking, there are two types of agencies:

- **The single agency** — In this type of agency, the agent represents only the buyer or the seller, not both. Therefore, buyer's agents only have a fiduciary responsibility to the buyers. They have the responsibility of promoting the buyer's interests and keeping all information confidential unless it is legally required to do so. When working with a single agency agent, he or she should not be passing any information to the seller without the investor's knowledge or permission.

- **The dual agency** — In a dual agency, the same agent represents both buyer and seller or two different agents from that agency represent the buyer and the seller. This creates a conflict of interest. The agent owes fiduciary loyalty to each client and this is difficult, if not impossible, to achieve even with the limitations described below:

Dual Agency Limitations

- The Agent should be objective in his or her dealings with the buyer and seller.

- The Agent should disclose items of importance to both the buyer and seller except:

  ° The Agent should not reveal that the buyer or seller is willing to pay/accept a price other than the one contained in the offer.

  ° The Agent should not reveal the buyer's or seller's motivation unless instructed to do so by that party.

  ° The Agent should not reveal any personal information unless instructed to do so by that party.

  ° The Agent should reveal the physical defects known about a piece of property to the buyer of the property.

To avoid this situation and work with an agent from a single agency. Brokers and agents like the dual agency arrangement because it generates more commissions when they can represent both sides of the transaction. Many states ban dual agencies. If a person is in a state that does not ban it, the law likely requires agents to disclose the dual relationship before taking on a client. However, it never hurts to ask upfront so it is known what type of agency is being dealt with.

Compensating the Broker or Agent

Earlier in the book, we discussed how real estate brokers and agents should be compensated in lease option deals. In other transactions, real estate agents or brokers are usually only compensated when a sale is made, and that provides motivation for them to see a transaction go through. Normally, their compensation is calculated as a percentage of the sales price of a property. These commissions vary according to the property and the size of the transaction:

- Five to six percent for individual residential properties

- Three to five percent for small multifamily and commercial properties

- One to three percent for larger investment properties

- Ten percent or more for raw land

On the whole, the commissions are split between the seller and the agent representing the buyer. In actual practice, the commission is paid to the broker who then gives a share to the agent based on employment or commission agreement.

Here is an important point to remember — commissions are not fixed. They are always negotiable. This fact can help keep costs down because commissions can be costly. However, also keep in mind that a really good agent will introduce an investor to many potentially profitable investments. It may be well while for an investor to pay the full commission to them. If paying commissions is unappealing, another route can be taken — become a licensed real estate agent. This eliminates half of the expense of commissions. An investor can then represent himself or herself in deals and reduce the expense of transactions.

Finding a Great Broker or Agent

Make sure that any broker or agent being worked with is a full-time professional. Avoid part-time agents. They tend to be amateurs and are not worth the money. In fact, they may end up costing the investor money and will definitely cost the investor time. Dedicated individuals should be handling investment goals. It is also a good idea to choose an agent or broker who is expert in the market the investor has chosen to concentrate on. If single family residential homes are being targeted, find agents or brokers who have demonstrated knowledge of those particular properties. Do not just accept an agent's or broker's word that he or she is well versed in the market. Ask for proof in terms of sales. Also, do not forget to verify the following important items:

- **Licensure** — The agent should be fully licensed. Verify this by checking with online state databases. This simple step makes sure there are no citations or disciplinary actions on his or her record. Also, verify the agent's broker is in full compliance with state regulations.

- **References** — Ask for several references from the agent or broker. These references should be in the geographical area. Get the names and numbers and then call all these individuals to get a rounded picture of the agent's professionalism.

- **Reputation** — A broker or agent's reputation can reflect on the investor so be sure anyone chosen has an excellent one. An agent with a great reputation enhances one's chances of success, especially in complicated or adversarial negotiations. Look for an agent with a reputation for honesty. When an agent or broker is straight forward with buyers and sellers, customers appreciate it and they let others know. The result is more prospects and business. Also, seek out agents or brokers who possess the qualities of fairness, integrity, and a considerable amount of patience. Patience is especially important in commercial/industrial property negotiations which can be complicated affairs with many business knots to untie.

- **Excellent communication skills** — Choose an agent or broker who demonstrates good listening skills and who keeps the investor up-to-date on transactions. He or she should always have time for the investor. Above all, he or she should listen carefully and be able to understand exactly what the needs are.

- **Strong interpersonal and negotiating skills** — Real estate deals are essentially about bringing people together and, hopefully, making everyone happy. Seek out agents or brokers who have the wit, charm, and patience to handle participants and move them toward the objective of the deal. Check out an agent's negotiating skills by asking former clients how well he or she handled bargaining sessions.

Once a great agent or broker is found, maximize the use of his or her expertise and contacts in the targeted market areas. Treat the agent or broker well and fairly. Be a dedicated and professional buyer. Remember, agents only get paid for closed deals; they do not want to waste time and lose money on phantom buyers. Also, remember close relationships with agents and brokers will give an investor the inside track on the best properties — the ones that do not always make it into the MLS listings or newspapers.

THE APPRAISER

The appraiser's job was over viewed earlier in the book. In this section, we will take a closer look at the role of the appraiser and how it affects a real estate business. As mentioned previously, the job of real estate appraisers is to evaluate a property and relay what condition it is in. They are licensed by the state. They are often independent contractors associated with appraisal firms headed by a Certified Appraiser or equivalent. They negotiate compensation with their firm. It is usually a percentage of the fee that the appraisal company charges their clients. Appraisers provide two great benefits: First, they can uncover hidden problems that could cost the investor money. This allows the investor to avoid the property or negotiate a lower price. Second, they can do the opposite – uncover hidden opportunities that can increase the return on an investment. An example would be a home or building that does not look that great cosmetically but is otherwise structurally sound. A good appraiser will alert an investor to the fact that a minimum investment on his or her part could lead to a significant increase in value. He or she can also provide a history of a particular geographic area and let the investor know if it is in the path of progress.

Most appraisers will provide a report in writing, although sometimes they simply do it orally. The reports generally consist of:

- A description of the property and its locale based on a visit to the property by the appraiser. He or she evaluates the condition, overall livability based on design, layout, and appeal to the market, and other external factors.

- An evaluation of the highest and best use of the land.

- An evaluation of sales of comparable properties as similar to the appraised property as possible.

- Information regarding current real estate activity and/or market area trends.

- New construction cost and analysis of income potential may be included in the report.

If a bank is being worked with, it may provide a list of approved appraisers that can be used. If not, any appraiser can be used. However, check to make sure the selected appraiser is not blacklisted by the bank. Some unethical appraisers inflate appraisal amounts and be can be blacklisted for this practice.

THE REAL ESTATE ATTORNEY

If a person is just starting out in lease options or other forms of real estate investment, he or she may not need an attorney. However, as the business grows, the services of an experienced real estate lawyer will definitely be needed. Investment transactions are complicated, and a good attorney can save a person money and hassle by reviewing all documents before a deal goes through. As with other members of the team, check references. Look for attorneys who have the knack of explaining legal terminology in plain English. They will be good communicators and make life easier. Also, seek out attorneys who have expert knowledge in leases, lease options, tenant-landlord laws, etc.

CONTRACTORS OR REPAIRMEN

As with other members of the team, the best and most experienced contractors or repairmen possible are desired. When deciding to upgrade properties, they may be needed in one or more of the following areas: heating and air conditioning, plumbing, electricity, roofing, carpet laying, painting, and general repair. For specialized areas, use only licensed contractors. These areas require extensive knowledge and experience and substandard work is not acceptable. It is a fact that unlicensed workers are often used for nonspecialized work simply because it costs less to use them. However, be aware that most insurance policies do not cover injuries to unlicensed workers. This mean an investor could end up incurring liability for damages. To find the best contractors and repairmen, ask around in the business community, check the "Services Available" section in the newspaper, or simply keep an eye out for repair trucks on the street. With contractors, be sure to check their references and license status. Talk to at least three customers who have used their services. Find out if they have done a quality job on time and within budget. Also, check with the Better Business Bureau to make sure there are no marks against their record.

22

ACTING AS A LANDLORD

This book has been primarily about buying and selling lease options on various properties. However, make no mistake, an investor is a landlord in many respects, especially if he or she decides to buy and hold a property. Particularly with multifamily dwellings, an investor needs to know what he or she is getting into in terms of landlording before committing to the profession. Success in the profession does require that a person possess certain qualities to begin with. In a way, landlords need to be a jack of all trades and master of every one of them. First of all, a landlord needs to be a people person who loves meeting with people, listening to them, and solving their problems. A landlord also has to be a numbers person. Software makes it much easier these days, but if a person is the landlord of a multiunit dwelling, for example, there are basic accounting functions that must be accomplished on a regular basis. And, it does not stop there — a landlord also has to be a handyman and love to maintain and repair things. In addition, it takes a lot of time and effort to be a landlord even beyond maintenance and repair problems. A landlord has to keep vacancies to a minimum, study the market, be aware of state laws, etc. On top of that, he or she will have to be available to tenants at odd hours of the day and night. Finally, landlord may have to deal with the public's false perception of the landlord as being a sketchy character — out to get money by squeezing every penny out of a property and renters. Every profession has its share of unethical people, but 99 percent of landlords are good, honest people who treat their renters well and enjoy what they are doing. And that same 99 percent realizes that the worst possible thing a landlord can do is mistreat tenants. That is because, in the long run, it is financial suicide. Once a landlord commits unethical acts, word-of-mouth kicks in, and soon, the pool of applicants dries up and so does his or her income. Smart, ethical landlords also realize that word-of-mouth is the best possible advertising they can get. When they create a great image for their properties, they will soon have a waiting list of applicants eager to rent and the income will continue to flow and increase. In short, integrity pays off both ethically and financially.

If a person feels he or she does not possess all the qualities listed above, then there are two choices. Avoid buying lease options on these properties or hire a property manager to manage the properties. The latter option assumes that a person is interested in a long-term, rather than short-term, investment strategy. It can be a great method of transitioning from lease optioning into building real estate wealth over a number of years. We will give advice on finding and hiring a professional property manager later in this chapter.

LANDLORDING

Basically, a landlord is a person who selects the best tenants available, collects rental payments, maintains the property, and administers records. In military terms, this is the "tactical level;" that is, the day-to-day work required to carry out a strategy. At a "strategic" level, the objective as a landlord is to lease option, buy, and maintain one or more properties in order to *create* a steady cash flow through rent. In the long run, a significant amount of wealth can be created with this strategy. That is because the landlord not only gets the cash flow, but increases his or her net worth over

CHAPTER 22 - ACTING AS A LANDLORD

the long haul. Traditionally, it has been the path to wealth for many, many creative and dedicated entrepreneurs.

Once a person has decided to become a landlord, the first questions to ask are these: "What type of properties should I lease option or invest in?" and "Which types can I realistically penetrate based on my knowledge and financial resources?" The answers to these questions should fit one's objectives for the lease option/real estate career. For those who are beginners and lack a considerable amount of financial resources, then it would not make sense to tackle the commercial or industrial markets. He or she would have to start on the lower end. To get a broad perspective on what types of properties may suit one's objectives, here is an overview of the typical properties available. There are eight common types of housing that are usually available in markets. Each type has its own advantages and disadvantages. Study them closely to determine where advantages outweigh disadvantages in terms of one's experience and resources.

- *Single residence occupancy buildings* (*SROs*) — In the early part of the 20th century, SROs were often known as "boarding homes" or "rooming" houses and often had a bad reputation. However, in today's market, they may be renovated properties aimed at special needs individuals and serve a good community purpose. Unlike their predecessors, today's SRO is likely to be a thoroughly modern building with fire sprinklers, handicapped access, and up-to-date facilities. They can be a good investment in terms of income, but, of course, government regulations have to be addressed. The older style SROs still exist. Often, they are older hotels, motels, or converted houses and are located in low income areas. They can be a good source of income, but may come with the considerable disadvantages of crime, vandalism, and obnoxious tenants. On the other hand, if a town has a large university or college with limited housing, an SRO can be a great and constant source of income as students are always looking for affordable places to stay.

215

- *Mobile homes/trailer parks* — Trailer parks sometimes have a negative reputation as places where "trailer trash" live. While that can be true, most mobile home residents are good people who simply lack the income to live in "stick-built" homes. This fact can translate into a reliable, steady income for an investor. The biggest headaches come in the form of maintenance and repair. It is a lot more difficult to maintain trailer homes than it is to maintain a single property. Problems multiply.

- *Low-end houses and duplexes* — Low-end houses were discussed earlier in the book in terms of under priced properties, but duplexes were not mentioned. They can be very profitable relative to other properties since there are two tenants paying rent on a monthly basis instead of just one. The disadvantages can be crime, damage to the property, and difficult renters. But these disadvantages can be avoided upfront by choosing a duplex in a quality neighborhood. All that is required is some homework.

- *Multiunit apartment dwellings* — Discussed earlier in the book, apartment buildings can be located in any part of town, from low-income to moderate-income to high-end neighborhoods. Their great advantage is that they can generate a significant amount of cash flow. A 50 unit building at $750 a month brings in $56,250 a month. However, this market requires considerable financial resources and knowledge, and is not for beginners. An additional disadvantage is turnover rate as people move out for various reasons. That means loss of income for the landlord. Another possibility, if remote, is that if the neighborhood declines, the landlord is stuck with a property that may be perceived as undesirable, and that, of course, also leads to loss of income.

- *Townhouses and condominiums* — Occupants of these properties tend to have stable incomes and life styles and are likely to remain as good sources of income. There are fewer people to deal with than in an apartment building. Fewer units also mean fewer maintenance and repair problems. On the down side, a landlord most likely will have to deal with a tenants' association. Such associations establish and enforce laws on items like parking, building, maintenance, lawn maintenance, pets, etc. If there is conflict between members, they will have to be settled.

- *Single family homes* — Although single family homes have been a focus of this book, there is another advantage that has not been previously mentioned — the spreading of financial risk. This means that an investor has the luxury of buying houses in different parts of the community. If one home is located in a neighborhood that is starting to decline, there are still properties in other neighborhoods in which homes are appreciating.

- *Commercial/industrial properties* — These properties were also discussed earlier in the book, but there are two more advantages to consider. One is that commercial/industrial tenants want success as much as the investor does, so they are likely to be highly responsible with the property. A second advantage is maintenance costs. Since the investor simply rents the building to these tenants, he or she normally is not responsible for property maintenance; the tenants are. That means the maintenance costs are virtually nil. However, Do not forget the disadvantages.

Commercial/industrial properties are closely linked to the economy. If the economy heads south, an investor can have an empty building for months or years and will still have to pay the mortgage. The investor will also have to work harder to find new tenants which can add up to thousands of dollars. In addition, the building may have to be renovated to meet the particular needs of a tenant's business.

- *Upper-income properties* — Luxury homes bring the highest income — and the most risk. For example, if the economy nose dives, owners often cannot afford the rent and head out the door in search of lower-income homes or apartments, leaving the investor with high mortgage costs until the economy recovers.

If an investor is a beginner in lease options or other areas of real estate, it is best to concentrate on single family homes and duplexes. It is more financially feasible and people always need a place to live no matter how bad the economy. It is not a free ride, of course. Vacancies will tend to be longer and the investor will have to work harder to find tenants. In addition, there may be more slow payers and that hassle will need to be addressed. However, that is a minor headache compared to receiving no income from commercial/industrial properties or high-income homes.

Okay, let us assume that an area of investment has been chosen and it is time to move on to the duties and responsibilities of being a landlord. They can be divided into two general areas — marketing the properties and maintenance and repairs. Let us look at marketing first.

MARKETING YOUR PROPERTIES

Properties without tenants are worthless. They are an absolute drag on one's financial resources. As a landlord, the first task is to attract tenants. To do that, it is helpful to adopt a manufacturer's state of mind. By that, we mean that manufacturers have a product to sell and they want to make it as attractive as possible to get the maximum number of buyers and create a profit. A landlord has a product as well and it should be as attractive as possible to tenants. It should be more attractive than the properties of any competitors. Remember, real estate consumers have many choices to make. Have any properties that are lease optioned or owned in the best possible shape before marketing them.

Marketing begins with advertising. Earlier in the book, methods of advertising lease optioned properties were discussed. In this section, we will take a more in-depth look at the subject as it relates to both lease options and "buy-to-hold" properties. The first principle to follow in marketing real estate is to target the advertising. Do not shotgun the approach and try to appeal to everyone in the area. It simply does not work and, therefore, is not cost effective. Instead, zero in on the type of renters that are desired in that single family home or in a multiunit dwelling. For example, if reliable, steady renters who will remain for a long period of time are sought, do not target young families; instead, aim for older individuals with established careers and incomes. It is illegal to discriminate against race, color, national origin, sex, family status, or disability. However, it is perfectly legal to direct advertising toward certain age groups or occupations. For example, if a property is close to several large corporations, the advertising can be directed toward middle managers and executives. Or, if a property is in a college town, word the ads to attract professors, university administrators, etc.

There are a number of ways in which properties can be marketed. Here is an overview of each:

- *Signage* — It is amazing the power a simple "For Rent" sign placed in the yard or on the building can have. According to the National Association of Realtors®, close to 88 percent of all homes are sold to drive-by customers. They investigate neighborhoods to see if they are suitable and ask their friends to keep an eye out for a suitable property or home. When opening a property to the public, the first order of business is to put up a sign. This is not a time to go cheap and stick up a hand lettered "For Rent" message. That approach sends a negative message to would-be renters. It says the landlord is an amateur and certainly not fussy about appearances. It sends the message that the property and/or units may be neglected or substandard and the tenants will not

219

be treated with care. Make sure the sign is professional and has as much curb appeal as the property itself. Hire a professional sign maker to create signs. Remember, it is a one-time expense and will pay off in tenants who provide long-term profitability. Also, remember to place the signs where they have the greatest visibility to the greatest amount of traffic on the road.

- *Classified advertisements* — Especially if a person has invested in "buy to hold" properties, it pays to expand beyond daily newspaper advertisements. Place ads in local newspapers and free shoppers. Select newspapers and shoppers which appeal directly to the renter audience. To do otherwise is to waste money. The most effective ads are short, sweet, and filled with words designed to appeal to the target audience. The following examples show words that fit the needs of specific customers:

    o *Older people* — secure, quiet, sheltered, close to walking trails, cozy

    o *Younger people* — inexpensive, large pool, modern exercise facilities, close to campus

    o *Married couples with children* — close to excellent schools, roomy, large backyard

In essence, the sales technique described earlier in the book is used — selling benefits and using them to build a positive image in the customer's mind. Make sure the ad is highly readable. Some real estate individuals cram their ads with every abbreviation imaginable, thinking that they are painting a wonderful picture for prospective customers. In reality, they usually end up painting a picture of confusion, forgetting that readers do not always know what the abbreviations mean. Too many abbreviations not only confuse readers but annoy them as well because they have to try to decipher what they mean. On the other hand, provide enough clear information in the ad about the property so the same items do not have to be described over and over again. To get a sense of effective ads, review the real estate section of the classifieds. See which ones catch are eye-catching and describe a property quickly and clearly. Then, use them as a model.

- *Rental guides* — Rental guides can be found in larger population, lower-income areas. They exist as a means for renters to make sense of the often bewildering array of rental possibilities. Rental guides put a convenient, thorough listing right in their hands and those listings are usually more up-to-date and detailed than the advertisements in newspapers. If a person has control of a multiunit dwelling, a rental guide can be a good choice, not only because of the targeted listings but also because the guide is free. It is all paid for by advertising. There is a second benefit as well. Rental guides have more room on the page than the classified section of the newspaper and that allows a landlord to get more information in the listing which, in turn, can help market the property to customers more effectively. As with any marketing method, there are disadvantages as well. Customers have to buy rental guides, so the marketing reach will not be as broad and this limits the pool of potential applicants. A second potential disadvantage is that unethical competitors sometimes list properties using the "bait and switch" technique; i.e., advertising luxury accommodations at bargain prices while only having regular apartments/duplexes, etc. available. The object is simply to lure customers in the door and then sell them on what is available. Needless to say, this creates unhappy customers. If a property is listed along with unethical landlords, those customers may see the landlord as guilty by association. The best way to prevent this is to read a rental guide before listing properties in it. A quick glance will tell if dubious practices are being followed by advertisers.

- **_Handbills_** — Handbills or flyers were mentioned earlier in the book. Here is more detail on the subject. First, the advantages: handbills are quick and cheap compared to classified or rental guide advertising. Using a computer, they can be created and produced easily. The downside of flyers is that they have to be distributed. The most effective method of distribution is to target the market just as with other forms of advertising. For example, if young couples with children are being targeted, then put the handbills up on bulletin boards where they are like to gather; e.g., community centers, supermarkets, etc. Go around to reputable merchants and ask permission to display handbills. Do not forget to keep track of the handbill-posting locations, so they can be taken down eventually. Leaving them up too long creates the idea that there's something wrong with the property.

- **_The Internet_** — Once multiple properties are acquired, an Internet site can be an effective marketing/advertising tool. It is inexpensive; it has broad reach; it can be customized to fit one's specific needs; and display photographs, floor plans, and maps to direct customers to the properties can be displayed. Those who are technologically inclined can create and maintain their own site. It is easy to do these days using web authoring software like Front Page or DreamWeaver. These applications use templates that make it easy to create a site. On the Internet, trial versions of such applications can often be downloaded for free. Whatever software is chosen, do not get caught up in the bells and whistles of an application and add fancy graphics that tax a customer's computer. Complex graphics make a site very slow to download on older computers and this makes potential customers very impatient. If the site is slow, they will move to a competitor's site in an instant. Keep the site attractive but simple. Viewers should be able to access key information as quickly as possible so they can be sold on the benefits of the properties. Also, as with other forms of advertising, target the audience. That means getting it indexed on the major search engines so potential customers can find the site. Enter "search engine optimization" in the search window and that should lead to information about optimization. However, be aware that there are scam companies who charge for SEO service and provide nothing. We recommend following Google's guidelines for choosing a provider.

Another method of using the Internet is to list vacancies on a site devoted to classified advertising in the area. To find these sites, run Internet searches on "classifieds" [town] and "apartments" for rent [town]. Check each site out carefully and avoid those with little or no classified advertising. Of course, the great advantage of the Internet is that a person can advertise nationwide with such services as:

- **ForRent.com**

- **Rent.com**

- Rentalhomesplus.com

One final word on the subject of advertising: Many landlords treat advertising as a one shot deal, Particularly with multiunit dwellings. This is a mistake. Vacancies cost money, and, if a building has them and no one knows about them, the landlord will definitely be losing money. Keep the properties constantly in the public eye. Advertise on a consistent and constant basis.

FINDING GOOD TENANTS

Every landlord wants the perfect tenant — a person who pays on time, never moves, and treats the property with respect. However, since all tenants are human beings, that means the perfect renter for properties will rarely be found. Different likes, dislikes, needs, and temperaments need to be dealt with. However, difficulties with renters can be reduced by planning ahead and establishing ground rules for the customers who will be accepted within the housing law guidelines. Here are the ground rules to use to find good tenants.

First of all, qualify the applicants. Doing this is a combination of asking good questions and using intuition about an applicant. Here is a suggested list of questions to ask:

- Where are you living now?

- How long have you lived there?

- Why do you want to move from there?

- Do you have enough money for the deposit?

- Do you have good credit?

- Have you ever been evicted or asked to move out?

- Do you smoke?

- Do you have pets?

People can and do lie when answering these questions. That is where the intuition comes in. Through experience, a landlord will develop a feel for when a person is telling the truth and when they are lying. At this point, some of these questions may seem pretty direct and blunt. If asking such questions makes a landlord uncomfortable, remember that the best possible tenants are desired. They are a source of income. Undesirable tenants end up causing grief and a loss of money. Develop a thick skin and ask those questions.

Assuming the right answers those initial questions are received, take the next step and inform the person that a credit check will be done and ask for their authorization. Ask them first what their credit rating is. Some may not know what it is. If they lie and say they have excellent credit and one of the credit reporting agencies sends a report with a low credit score, then this person is not the right tenant.

Depending upon the area in which the properties are located, consider doing a criminal background check. This also requires written authorization by the prospective tenant. If the person hangs up or leaves quickly, then an undesirable tenant has just been screened.

Before calling previous landlords for a recommendation on the people applying for the property, it never hurts to ask what they think that former landlord will say about them. Their response can tell a landlord volumes about their suitability as tenants.

SHOWING THE PROPERTY

Okay, let us assume that some prospects have been qualified. The next step is to show the property. Explain where the property is and, if they are driving separately, give clear directions. Then, show the property by highlighting its good features while being honest about any problems and the neighborhood. If the landlord has done his or her job upfront by asking the prospective renters about their likes and dislikes and have selected the property to meet their needs, this should not be a problem. Simply remember that it is a waste of time to try to shove a property on them that the landlord knows they are going to reject.

Another good, and more efficient, method of showing a property is to hold an open house. Showing the property to several people at once has great benefits for a landlord. It saves time and money and, at the same time, it creates a buyer's atmosphere. It is human nature for interest to rise when several people attend an open house. They get competitive, and that puts the landlord in the driver's seat in terms of the amount of rent that can be charged.

Whether an open house or an individual showing is held, this is an opportunity for the landlord to judge the prospects as potential renters. The remarks they make, the way they treat the property, the way they treat the landlord — these are all clues as to how they will behave as tenants and will help in making the right decision. Be sure to offer applications to all who attend a showing. And be sure to tell them that all applications will be reviewed. This demonstrates that a landlord is methodical and nondiscriminatory in the application process.

The next step is to *review the applications*. Application forms do not need to be complicated affairs, but they should ask for certain basic information. This includes:

- Name, address, and telephone number
- Date of birth
- Driver's license number
- Social security number
- Current and past tenancies
- Current and past job history
- Financial status
- Number of occupants to be in the property
- Pets

Along with the application, provide instructions on how to fill it out. Do not forget to ask each person to fill out an application if there is going to be more than one occupant. For example, if a husband and wife are applicants or there are two roommates, they should each fill out an application. This creates more paperwork, but it also protects the landlord against discrimination while, at the same time, it provides good information to use in case a renter decides to skip out.

Review each application and use common sense. If applicants have not provided previous addresses or job histories are sketchy, then a red flag should go up. A landlord does not want to rent a valuable piece of property to people hiding their backgrounds. Plus, unwittingly, these individuals have eliminated themselves at minimum time and cost to the landlord.

Once the applicants are reviewed and desirable tenants are found, check their references. If they are legitimate and the applicants are given a good rating, act quickly. Remember, there is competition for good tenants, so there is no time to waste in nailing down a rental agreement. Make a signing appointment. When applicants arrive for the meeting, explain the agreement to them point by point to make it clear from the start what is expected of them as renters and of the landlord. This can prevent misunderstandings down the road. During the explanation process, do not be afraid to ask the applicants for their understanding of such points as deposits, vacating notices, and other major items. First of all, it is a great method of checking to make sure they do actually understand. If they do not, then explain the point to them again. Second, it is a good way of firmly planting the conversation in both parties' memories so if disputes arise later, the landlord can remind them that those specific points were discussed during the meeting.

After a thorough explanation of the rental agreement, have the applicants sign the form and request a deposit and a minimum of the first month's rent. If more than one month's rent can be acquired, go for it.

Now that the tenants have been signed it is time to move them in and that is the subject of the next section.

MOVING YOUR TENANTS IN

When moving tenants in, it is a great time to establish a good relationship with them. They are customers, after all, and a landlord wants them to be steady, rent paying tenants for years, if possible. To establish that good relationship, take the following steps:

First, inspect the property thoroughly before the tenants move in. Fix what needs to be fixed and have the place as clean and sparkling as possible. This helps create a good impression of the property and of the landlord as well. Second, when the tenants move in, go through the property thoroughly with them with the manager's checklist. The checklist should list all the items in the property and the conditions of those items. This procedure is important because it allows the landlord to deal with any problems immediately and prevents them from turning into sources of complaint later. It also prevents disagreements about the condition of the place at the end of the leasing term. When going through the list, ask the tenants to initial the items and sign the form. Most importantly, if something needs to be replaced or repaired and the landlord promises to do it, be sure to follow through on that promise and fix it as quickly as possible. That demonstrates to the tenants that the landlord keeps his or her word and wants them to have the best experience possible. They will then tell their friends about this honesty and commitment and word-of-mouth will bring in more business.

During the move-in procedure, do not forget to mention the inspection procedures. Tell tenants that the landlord will check back with them on a scheduled basis to make sure they are satisfied with the property and to fix any problems. This shows that there will not be an absentee landlord. It also allows the landlord to check the condition of the property and to spot any problems that might have cropped up in the meantime. After all, a landlord does not want drug dealers or hard partiers damaging property and offending other renters or neighbors.

One last note for this section: At the time of move in, recommend to tenants that they get renter's insurance so they are covered in case of fire, theft, and other damages. It is inexpensive insurance and worth every penny in terms of protecting assets.

Now that there are tenants in the property, it is important to retain them. That is the subject of the next section.

RETAINING GOOD TENANTS

Think of good tenants as an investment in the future. They are a steady source of income and can help one reach his or her financial goals. Also think of the flip side of the coin: When tenants leave, there are vacancies. Vacancies cost money, time, and trouble. Retention of good tenants should be one of the primary goals as a landlord. Right from the start, write out a tenant retention program with that goal in mind. Here are a few low cost and free suggestions that can do wonders in making tenants appreciate the landlord and want to continue to live in the properties.

- *Memorize names* — This is the most basic way of helping to keep good tenants and it is free. Good tenants are paying good money and they expect the landlord to know their names. If the time is not taken to learn their names, they feel the landlord does not have time for them at all and simply does not care. And if no commitment is shown to them, they will not feel any commitment to the landlord. They may seek a friendlier place, and that puts a hit on the bottom line.

- *Listen, listen, listen* — This is another free and basic skill, but it is important. Everyone likes to feel their concerns and problems are being heard. It comes down to making tenants feel as if the landlord knows them individually. Here are a few simple tricks to make people think you know them. First, look them in the eye when they are talking and provide them with full attention. Do not be doing other things at the same time like filling out forms. Second, nod during the conversation and say phrases like "I see," "I understand," "Is that right?" Third, summarize what they said. It could be something sympathetic like, "Mary, I am sorry your faucet of leaking. You would like it fixed by Tuesday. Is that right?" Of course, any property is going to have its share of bores with frivolous complaints as well as legitimate concerns. But, through practice, a landlord will learn to keep them happy and satisfied while limiting conversation with them. And, remember, a bore is still paying rent.

- *Hire tenants* — This is a good idea if there are handyman-type tenants. They appreciate the money or deduction from the rent, enjoy the work, and take more pride in the building and the grounds because they now have a personal investment.

- *Redecorate for good, long-term tenants* — Be sure to keep track of the condition of apartments or houses for good tenants. These properties should be as attractive as possible to retain these tenants. Offer to redecorate the place if it has not been done for a while. They may be perfectly happy with the current condition of the place, but they will definitely appreciate the offer.

- *Move-in gifts* — These are items that brighten up a living space and show the new tenants that they are welcome and their business is appreciated. Such gifts can include thank you baskets, flowers, memo pads with pens and pencils, and other inexpensive items.

- *Holiday/birthday cards* — Send tenants cards for Christmas, Hanukah, other religious holidays, marriages, and for birthdays, etc. It shows that the landlord is thinking of them.

- *Lease renewal gifts* — With multiunit properties, this is a method of reminding tenants that their business is still appreciated and their presence is enjoyed. Gifts can include ceiling fans, new blinds, carpet cleaning, and other such items. This is a win-win gift. The tenants appreciate them, and, at the same time, it increases the value of the property. The longer the tenant stays, the more the value of the gift should increase.

- *Incentive programs* — Offer a long-term tenant $50 or $100 off on their first month's rent after the lease is renewed.

- *Referral fees* — This is a low cost prospecting tool for a landlord and the prospecting is done by the tenant Offer a $25 or $50 referral fee to a good tenant. Word-of-mouth referrals are especially powerful coming from long-term tenants because they will say good things about the landlord and the properties.

There will come a time when a good tenant needs to leave. After all, circumstances change. But be sure to ask them specifically why they are leaving and make sure it is not because of some problem with the property that the landlord is not aware of. If there is a problem, it may be taken care of it and a tenant may not be lost.

Whatever the cause, if they have definitely decided to leave, then be sure to talk to them personally and wish them well. Remember, they will tell others how they were treated so it is good business sense to treat them with respect. In fact, use the situation as an opportunity to ask them if they know of anyone who would like the vacated space. They may have friends or relatives who are looking for a place.

With good tenants in multiunit dwellings, another issue that will have to be dealt with is rent increases. No one likes rent increases, of course, but landlords especially do not want good tenants upset at paying more money on a weekly or monthly basis. This situation calls for a personalized letter. In the letter, first explain why the rent is being increased. Do not just say it is being raised. There are reasons behind the increase and those reasons need to be explained to tenants. Rent increases are usually due to increased costs in energy costs, taxes, inflation, and other economic facts of life. Tenants may not be happy about this, but they understand those facts.

But do not just stop at explaining the rent increase. Tie it to a reward. Tell the tenant, "We are going to clean your carpet and put in new blinds as a small measure of our thanks for your continued patronage." Rewards like that take some of the sting out of the rent increase.

Reduce complaints from good tenants by keeping their rent a few dollars below what new tenants are charged. This tactic shows that they are being given special consideration and they will appreciate the gesture. Further reduce the complaints about rent increases by preparing all tenants for the increase ahead of time. Simply let it be known that the costs have risen to due to economic conditions and rent will need to be raised at some point. Next, let tenants know exactly when the rent will increase so they can adjust to the idea. There will be some initial grumbling, but eventually it will die down as they accept the fact of the increase. Give them at least 30 days notice of a rent increase. Even better, 60 days gives more time for the idea to be accepted.

Over time a landlord's rent increases as well. If possible, tie it to some improvement to the properties. Maybe have the exterior painted, the swimming pool refurbished, or the grounds improved. If so, time the rent increase so it occurs with those improvements. That gives tenants visible proof that their rent increase is actually providing them with a benefit.

It is time to go deeper into the subject of rent and rent collection and rent collection procedures are the subject of our next section.

COLLECTING RENT

As a landlord, certain qualities will be needed to collect rent. First, he or she needs to be consistent and have a consistent system set up to collect that rent so tenants know exactly when their rent is due. This is not an area to be haphazard.

The best way to be consistent is to have a computerized rental tracking system. This software can be found on the Internet by doing a search.

Possibilities include RentTracker.com or Rental Property Tracker Plus (**http://productivity-software.comrental/**). Or a system can be set up using readily available financial management software like QuickBooks. The basic goal of the rent collection system is simple — at any given time, a landlord should be able to look at the screen or a printout and tell what percentage of the rent has been collected as of that date. That way, the late payers can be identified can be targeted.

Be persistent and firm with those tenants who do pay late. They signed an agreement and are occupying valuable property. It is their responsibility to pay on time. If a tenant is late, contact them and remind them of the agreement and, at the same time, explain the collection procedures. For example, assume rent is collected on the first of the month. Tell the offending tenant that rent is considered late if it is not paid by the fifth of the month and that the landlord will be paying them a visit by the sixth if the money and the late penalty fee are not forthcoming.

Have a standard collection procedure in place when the business is started. It can help reduce the number of late payers because they understand the policy from the moment they sign an agreement. The policy should include the following items:

- A standard collection procedure

- Specified form of payment

- Written receipts

- A set rental due date

- A set late payment date

- Late payment penalty

Each landlord's situation is different or he or she will need to adapt collection procedures to fit that situation. It all depends upon the type of tenants, the number of units, where the landlord lives in relation to the units, how much he or she wants to be involved, and whether or not there is an on-site manager. The landlord may have the tenants come to the office or a manager's office to drop off their rent checks. The rent may be collected by mail or have a drop box. Of course, the rent can always be collected in person, but this is probably the least efficient method. Depending on the number of properties or apartment units, it eats up valuable time and can cost money in terms of transportation costs. There is an upside to this method, however. It establishes the landlord's presence to the renters and shows them that he or she cares enough to make sure the property is in good shape. It also allows the landlord to take care of any problems that might have cropped up in the time since the last rent payment.

When collecting late rents, consider the people from whom the rent is being collected. If tenants have been good payers and are suddenly late, it may be simply because they forgot, were sick, or had a death in the family. Such tenants deserve patience and understanding.

On the other hand, chronically late paying tenants deserve nothing but firmness. They are costing the landlord money and not living up to a legal agreement. Visit them personally and be blunt. Tell them that they need to pay on time all the time or the agreement will have to be terminated and the property/apartment will be put up for rent for tenants who do pay on time. This kind of toughness is important, not only for the individual tenant concerned, but also because it sets an example for other tenants who might be inclined to pay late.

An alternative to collecting late rent payments is to use collection attorneys. The advantage of this approach is that it takes collection procedures out of the landlord's hands and puts it in the hands of professionals. The disadvantage is that the attorneys may charge up to a third of what they collect as well as court fees.

A better approach may be to recommend a list of social, religious, and governmental agencies who are dedicated to helping out individuals who are short on income. This approach creates a better image than using collection attorneys. Use judgment in this area. If the tenants are honest, hard working people who are simply in a bad situation, then recommend the "helping-hand" agencies. If the tenants are simply low-lifes who make it a habit to avoid payment, then choose the collection agency route.

That brings us to the least pleasant aspect of being a landlord — evictions.

A REVIEW OF EVICTION PROCEDURES

Eviction is a legal procedure that must be followed to the letter. Tenants cannot simply be tossed out on the street. The only person who can actually move a person out of a property is a sheriff or other duly-appointed officer of the law. Remember also that legally a landlord cannot do the following:

- Throw them out of the dwelling

- Turn off their gas, electricity, or water to get them to move

- Take their belongings

- Harass them

- Threaten them with bodily harm

Ethically, these things should not be done in the first place no matter how obnoxious the tenant has been. These actions will set a landlord up for lawsuits and fines that can cost much more than the rent lost to a bad tenant. For more details on the subject, review the fair housing laws covered earlier in the book or go to **Fairhousinglaw.org** or to the Housing and Urban Development (HUD) site at **http://www.hud.gov/**.

Hopefully, a landlord will not have to do many evictions, but here are the procedures to follow. First, there are two choices in eviction proceedings. A landlord can do it or a specialist can be hired to do it — an eviction/collection attorney. Doing it personally is cheaper and faster. On the other hand, hiring an attorney protects a landlord against being sued by a bad tenant. Also, eviction laws are different in every state so the attorney will more likely be aware of the technicalities. However, an attorney is more expensive and will be slower which costs a landlord money in rent from new tenants.

The first step in eviction proceedings is to serve a notice of eviction. To meet legal requirements, it must be properly filled out and properly served. The notice should state the following information:

- The number of days tenants have in which to comply to the order

- The names of all the tenants in the property

- The address of the rental dwelling

- The amount of rent due

- The period for which rent is due

- Date of the notice

- The landlord's signature

It is better to serve the notice in person rather than mail it because longer waiting periods may apply for mailed notices. A landlord can serve it or he or she can hire another person for the job, someone who is tough enough to handle potentially bad circumstances. If a person is hired, make sure they understand the legal aspects of eviction and are not going to do anything illegal. Whenever possible it is best to perform evictions quickly and cleanly.

Now, let us turn our attention to a more pleasant topic and a large part of a landlord's duties — maintenance and repair.

MAINTENANCE AND REPAIR

For a landlord, the downside of maintenance and repair is the fact that costs can eat up profits and cause considerable exasperation. The upside is that it is an opportunity to show good tenants that the landlord is committed to giving them a good rental experience and is paying attention to their needs. Remember, a good tenant experience creates good word-of-mouth, and that, in turn, brings more business. It is best to look on the positive side while attempting to keep maintenance and repair costs to a minimum.

Appliances are a major source of expense. In the first place, they cost a lot to replace. In the second place, they are expensive to repair. A service call plus parts can cost hundreds of dollars. This expense means the cost of these appliances needs to be built into the rent. Or, in some cases, tenants can be encouraged to bring or buy their own appliances.

Repair costs can be high as well. Carpets need replacing, faucets leak, and plumbing bursts in cold weather. The best way to keep these costs to a minimum is to do preventive maintenance. Check the condition of fixtures, furnaces, and other items prior to a move-in and on a regular basis with all tenants. Depending on the number of properties owned, a landlord can do repairs if he or she is the handyman type. Or, if there is a manager, have him or her fix items.

And speaking of handymen, consider offering a deduction in rent to tenants who are good at repairs. Establish a maximum amount for minor repairs and offer them $10 or more off the rent in exchange for their services. Handyman types enjoy the work anyway and will love a reduction in rent.

A good idea is to have a three to five day policy in effect for maintenance and repairs. This tells tenants that the landlord is responsible and will meet their needs in a timely fashion.

In a related topic, damage to the property can occur either intentionally or unintentionally. The tenant is responsible for this damage and should pay for it. Tenants should be made aware of this policy at the time of the rental agreement signing, so they can be reminded of this fact when damage occurs. That will undercut their argument that the landlord should pay for it.

PROTECTING YOUR INVESTMENTS

The importance of protecting investments with the proper insurance cannot be stressed enough. Especially if being a landlord is one's entire livelihood, catastrophic losses due to fire, bad weather, or liability suits will be devastating. Compared to those major expenses, insurance costs are a bargain. If multiunit dwellings are owned, be sure to consider the vital types of insurance listed on the next page.

There are other types of insurance available and they may be appropriate. If properties are managed, get management insurance so suits do not have to be handled; the insurer does it instead. Another type of coverage is called an umbrella policy. Its name comes from the fact that it provides added liability protection above and beyond the limits of other insurance policies. It goes into effect when the liability on other polices has been exhausted. With an umbrella policy, an additional one to five million in liability protection can be received. If there are employees and/or contractors, workers compensation insurance is also excellent protection to have. This protects against frivolous lawsuits generated by accidents on the job.

Due to the litigious nature of our society, it is also wise to have legal protection in place to not only defend against lawsuits but also to deal with insurance companies averse to paying in the case of covered damages. There are two courses in this regard. One, retain a good lawyer who specializes in such matters. This is usually the best course because there is a personal relationship with the lawyer. However, if the expense is too much, opt for pre-paid legal services. Such services are inexpensive and they charge a monthly fee in the range of $10 to $30 a month. Check with the American Prepaid Legal Services Institute online at **http://www.aplsi.org/** for a partial listing of plans and services. Or try **PrePaidLegal.com**. This company covers civil cases or work related criminal cases.

Finally, do not forget the most important of all documents — one's will. In the event of death, a landlord wants his or her whole investment portfolio to go to family, relatives, or designated individuals and not to the government. If there is no will, the government steps in and can take a third of the assets before the estate is settled.

TYPES OF INSURANCE

- **Boiler/machinery insurance** — If a large multiunit, commercial, or industrial property is owned, this is prudent coverage to have. Boiler explosions can be devastating to both people and property. With this insurance, an added bonus is that the insurer will inspect the equipment on a regular basis. In effect, there is a partner in maintenance and safety.

- **Business interruption insurance** — This can be called "loss of rent" coverage. For example, assume water or fire damage one of the properties, and it cannot be occupied for any length of time. That means rent will be lost until it is repaired. All the while, fixed expenses keep piling up. Business interruption insurance prevents this because the insurance company compensates for the loss of rental income over a specified period.

- **Earthquake coverage** — For those living in an earthquake-prone area, this coverage is a must. Nature can damage or destroy a building in seconds. This is always a separate coverage.

TYPES OF INSURANCE

- **Extended coverage** — Common terms for this form of insurance are "comprehensive" coverage or a "package policy." Extended coverage protects from damage caused by hail, windstorms, smoke, rioting, falling trees, vandalism, freezing temperatures, landslides, and accidental water discharge from burst pipes. It is often offered along with the standard fire insurance policy and it is an investment well worth paying for. Fit the coverage to the particular geographic area.

- **Fire insurance** — This is not an area to neglect. Insure properties for top value or the insurance company may discount its payment. For example, if $100,000 is paid for a house and it is worth $200,000, but it is insured for only $180,000, then that $180,000 is all that will be received.

- **Flood insurance** — For those living in a flood-prone area, do not tempt the fates by neglecting to have the appropriate insurance. Floods do serious damage to buildings and the clean-up is long, messy, and costly. Remember, that insurers categorize flood damage as different from water damage caused by burst pipes and such, so extended coverage will not apply in flood situations.

- **Liability insurance** — This is an absolute necessity. However, read the policy closely to note any exclusions. You do not want to get a nasty surprise when you make a claim. It may be worth the extra expense to have any exceptions included in the insurance. If you do any building, remodeling, or painting, consider buying a separate contractor's insurance policy.

- **Mortgage insurance** — When trouble knocks on your door, this insurance pays off the balance of your outstanding mortgage. The price is worth it. Work with a lender to get the proper type for your needs.

TYPES OF INSURANCE

- **Property improvements insurance** — If you own or plan to own a large multiunit dwelling, a standard building policy will not cover damage to such items as swimming pools, fences, signs, parking lots, and other areas. Bad weather and extreme changes in temperature can severely damage these items, so make sure they are covered.

- **Title insurance** — Discussed earlier in the book, title insurance makes clear who owns the title and prevents you from throwing away money on a property that might legally belong to someone else.

- **Vandalism/malicious mischief** — This type of insurance is relatively inexpensive insurance and well worth the price. It pays for repair of damage and destruction caused vandals.

LANDLORD FORMS AND RESOURCES

As the size and scope of the properties increase, so will the number of forms that will be required. Luckily, the Internet can simplify the paper shuffle. Order forms from **Landlord.com** or at **mrlandlord.com**. There are other sites available too, which are specific to states. In print, there are many good sources of information on landlording as well as forms. One is Robert Shemin's *Secrets of a Millionaire Landlord*. It is a good primer on landlording and is easy to read. Leigh Robinson's *Landlording* is a more comprehensive book. It covers the topic in great detail and has extensive forms that can be used. Its many references on landlording will help increase one's knowledge of the field.

THE PROFESSIONAL MANAGEMENT OPTION

Hiring a professional property/real estate manager is a logical step as investments in the real estate field are grown. That is because an investor should be concentrating his or her efforts on increasing income and overall worth instead of dealing with the day-to-day details of landlording. It is simply a matter of choosing effectiveness over efficiency. A professional property manager takes the burden of tactical operations off a landlord's shoulders and allows him or her to focus on the big picture — creating a safe and profitable future. A property/real estate manager "oversees the performance of income producing commercial or residential properties and ensures that real estate investments achieve their expected revenues" (U.S. Bureau of Labor Statistics).

PROPERTY MANAGER DUTIES

Source: Bureau of Labor Statistics U.S. Department of Labor, Occupational Outlook Handbook, 2006-07 Edition, Property, Real Estate, and Community Association Managers, on the Internet at **http://www. bls.gov/oco/ocos022.htm**.

Often, property managers negotiate contracts for janitorial, security, groundskeeping, trash removal, and other services. When contracts are awarded competitively, managers solicit bids from several contractors and advise the owners on which bid to accept. They monitor the performance of contractors and investigate and resolve complaints from residents and tenants when services are not properly provided. Managers also purchase supplies and equipment for the property and make arrangements with specialists for repairs that cannot be handled by regular property maintenance staff.

Onsite property managers are responsible for the day-to-day operations of a single property, such as an office building, a shopping center, a community association, or an apartment complex. To ensure that the property is safe and properly maintained, onsite managers routinely inspect the grounds, facilities, and equipment to determine whether repairs or maintenance is needed. In handling requests for repairs or trying to resolve complaints they meet not only with current residents, but also with prospective residents or tenants to show vacant apartments or office space.

PROPERTY MANAGER DUTIES

Onsite managers also are responsible for enforcing the terms of rental or lease agreements, such as rent collection, parking and pet restrictions, and termination-of-lease procedures. Other important duties of onsite managers include keeping accurate, up-to-date records of income and expenditures from property operations, and submitting regular expense reports to the asset property manager or owners. Property managers who do [work offsite] act as a liaison between the onsite manager and the owner. They also market vacant space to prospective tenants through the use of a leasing agent or by advertising or other means and they establish rental rates in accordance with prevailing local economic conditions.

Some property and real estate managers, often called real estate asset managers, act as the property owners' agent and adviser for the property. They plan and direct the purchase, development, and disposition of real estate on behalf of the business and investors. These managers focus on long-term strategic financial planning, rather than on day-to-day operations of the property.

The key element in that statement is, of course, "achieve . . . expected revenues." That is exactly what a property manager should do — maintain and increase revenues. The choice of such a person or firm is extremely important. In general, property managers/firms handle the financial operations of properties: collect rent, pay mortgages, taxes, insurance premiums, payroll, and maintenance bills on time, etc. Some property managers are called asset property managers. They supervise the preparation of financial statements and periodically report to the owners on the status of the property, occupancy rates, expiration dates of leases, and other matters.

The choice of a property manager/firm is critical. Good ones increase profits and maintain the integrity of the property. Poor ones can be a financial disaster because they will cost a landlord money, not only in profits, but also in maintenance of the property. They can do this in a variety of ways – neglect the buildings and grounds, lease to unsuitable tenants, fail to uphold rules, and regulations, etc.

Once a contract is agreed to with a property management firm, that company will be granted the right and ability to make emergency repairs without advance notice from the landlord. Of course, the landlord will specify the limits of those repairs as part of the contract. It may range from $300 to $500 for a smaller property. With a larger one, that limit might be $2,000 to $3,000. Whatever the limit, make it very clear that it is a requirement that the company keep the landlord up to date on any expenses incurred.

In the beginning, monitor the property manager/firm's activities and expenses very closely. This prevents them from making unneeded repairs. Some less scrupulous firms use this tactic to make money. Management firms get paid in one of three ways: a percentage of the collected income, a flat fee on a monthly basis, or a dollar amount per unit per month for the entire property. The first option is normally the best choice. A percentage provides an incentive for the company to keep rents at market value as well as enforce rent collection. Management fees run around eight to ten percent for the management of single-family homes, condos, or small rental properties. The management fees for medium-sized properties fall in the range of six to eight percent. Large residential properties management fees are generally in the three to five percent range. The fees for management of commercial, industrial, or retail spaces run higher due to the fact that it takes considerable time and effort to find and qualify new tenants when an old tenant leaves. The property manager has to get the space ready and show it to prospective clients. In this case, the management commission is usually a percentage of the gross rent. It is often based on a sliding scale; the longer the lease, the lower the percentage in later years. In the case of residential rentals, the charge may either be a flat fee or a percentage of the monthly rental rate.

SELECTION AND INTERVIEW GUIDELINES FOR PROPERTY MANAGERS/FIRMS

• Interview several property managers to ensure they are qualified for the job. Compare their personalities, ease with people, ability to enforce rules and regulations in a sensitive way, etc. Avoid dictator types who have a "my way or the highway approach" that is certain to offend long-term tenants. Also, avoid the other extreme where the applicant wants to please tenants at any cost. A good property manager/firm is even-handed and objective.

• Check references of the interviewees by making the necessary phone calls.

• Review the company's track record for management of properties. Require that a list of their clients be provided, then follow up on that list by contacting rental owners for information.

• Ask for proof of licensing. Depending on the state, a property manager should have a real estate license, a property manager's license, or both. Good applicants will have this proof at hand and will be eager to provide it. Ask for professional accreditation from the Institute of Real Estate Management (IREM). This is an organization of professionals providing designation in three areas:

    o CPM — Certified Property Manager

    o ARM — Accredited Residential Manager

    o AMO — Accredited Management Organization

• Require proof of insurance. This is an absolute necessity. Any reputable property management company will carry insurance for general liability, automobile liability, worker's compensation, and professional "errors and omissions" insurance. Also, ensure that it has a substantial fidelity bond. The bond protects the landlord in the event an employee mishandles or embezzles money. If a firm cannot provide proof of insurance, run the other way.

SELECTION AND INTERVIEW GUIDELINES FOR PROPERTY MANAGERS/FIRMS

- Separate accounting. Any management firm will have separate accounting for each of its managed properties instead of a master trust account where funds from several clients are mixed together. This can lead to financial complications. So-called "creative" accounting can cost a landlord lots of money and legal troubles.

23

TAKING ACTION

————

A person can have all the best ideas in the world on lease optioning, but those ideas mean nothing if they are not put into action. The following steps are recommended to make the dream of financial independence come true. These steps do not necessarily go in order; some will be done simultaneously.

STEP 1: REVIEW/REVISE YOUR ACTION PLAN

Now that all the material in this book has been studied, go back to Chapter 4 and review the initial action plan. Is it still relevant based on what has been learned? If not, draft another one — and another until it is just right. This will ensure that an investor keeps on target with his or her goals — and takes action on objectives to achieve those goals.

STEP 2: "SWOT" YOURSELF

Do an objective analysis of personal strengths and weaknesses in terms of skills, knowledge, and attitude. A standard and effective method of doing this is called a SWOT analysis, which stands for "Strengths, Weaknesses, Opportunities, and Threats." It is a method that guides a person in an honest analysis of his or her personal strengths and weaknesses. This allows a person to maximize opportunities and avoid or get rid of potential threats. The analysis will help answer questions like:

- **What do I do well right now?** Really hone in on what one's expertise is. It is important to pinpoint these skills because people pay for expertise. Research to gain expertise or build on what has already been done. For example, if a person wants to concentrate on lease options, then plan on reading or viewing all the current information on that field. Also, join the local real estate investors group. This is a great way to gain specific knowledge and, hopefully, a mentor. In general, work out a plan to acquire all the specific lease option and real estate expertise that will be needed. And do not stop there — keep on learning every day. It is a characteristic of successful entrepreneurs that they never stop learning. They know they have to stay on top of developing opportunities and be ready to exploit them on a moment's notice.

- **Are there skills I am pretty good at now but would like to do better?** Just like athletes, we all need to take basic skills and hone them to a higher level in order to achieve the success we want and deserve. If a person has good skills, make them better. Read, join the appropriate groups, find a mentor, etc. For example, at the present time, a person may do well at public speaking, but wants to improve to be polished and professional in all interactions with customers and other real estate individuals. In that case, join the local Toastmasters group. It is not only a great way to polish speaking skills; it is also a means of building a circle of contacts as well as a reputation within the community.

- **What areas of skills, knowledge, and attitude do I really need to improve?** We all have weaknesses; it is part of being human. But it is a great drag on one's career if those weaknesses are dwelled on. The right course is to resolve to get rid of them. A person may already have an idea of his or her weaknesses. But some objective feedback from others is needed on the subject. To do this, ask for "360 degree" feedback; that is, simply ask trusted family members, friends, business associates, etc. They will help a person build a complete picture. Particularly if a person is beginning a real estate career, this helps get rid of obstacles that might impede the progress of that career. And these weaknesses can actually be turned into strengths. For example, trusted others may tell a person that they feel he or she could be a better listener. Since listening is a crucial skill in any business venture, lay out a plan to improve that skill.

- **What and how am I currently learning?** Knowledge is crucial to any endeavor. Specific knowledge of real estate is even more crucial to one's success. To build expertise in that area, attend seminars and workshops. Read trade journals and Web sites. Listen to audiotapes or CDs and watch videos/DVDs. Talk to mentors and experts in the field. In short, constantly seek new knowledge and new ideas to stay ahead of the competition.

- **What bad habits or traits do I have that I must modify or eliminate before I begin my real estate career?** Again, talk to trusted others to find out what one's bad habits or traits are. Get rid of them fast since they can hurt or slow one's career. For example, maybe a person fidgets excessively when talking to people or does not make eye contact. These bad habits can create a negative impression.

SWOT ANALYSIS EXAMPLE	
Strengths	**Weaknesses**
I communicate well with others.	Lack of capital.
I have the support of my family and loved ones.	Lack of sales training.
I am absolutely committed to success in the field of lease options.	Tend to wander off subject during business conversations; need to come to the point in a more professional and polished manner.
I demonstrate professionalism in all my business activities.	
I look and can act professionally.	
Opportunities	**Threats**
I can take advantage of the current market.	I tend to get discouraged easily if things do not go my way.
I have a good circle of contacts and friends in the business who can help me (and whom I can help).	Lack of financial knowledge puts me at a disadvantage compared to other real estate professionals.

At the end of the chapter, there is a blank example of a SWOT Analysis.

STEP 3: SET UP YOUR OFFICE

Earlier in the book, we provided the basics of office set-up. Use that information to gather the necessary materials, services, and equipment.

STEP 4: BEGIN A PORTFOLIO

A beginner may not have photos of homes, testimonials, and other important marketing materials, but he or she needs to acquire these items as soon as possible. It is important to have something tangible to show customers. Work on gathering them and then prepare a thoroughly professional portfolio. Remember, it is just as much a part of one's image as a professional as one's dress and manner of speech.

STEP 5: DO YOUR RESEARCH AND MAKE YOUR CONTACTS

Read the newspapers, online sites, home magazines, etc. and look for "For rent" and "For sale" ads to get an idea of the opportunities in the market. Then, once leads have been identified, talk to them. Do not get discouraged when turned down or feel there was a miscommunication. That is all part of the process. Think of it as honing skills because that is exactly what it is. And do not forget to reach out and talk to realtors. Introduce oneself to them and let them know the benefits an investor can provide them. If necessary, educate them on lease options in a pleasant and professional way. Ask them about their current listings and if any sellers have indicated that they might consider renting if the home does not sell soon. And follow up with another call or letters.

STEP 6: WRITE PROPOSALS

Writing good proposals takes practice, so beginners in the field should try writing five to ten mock proposals at first. Be sure to write them for different offers — cash out, lease option, seller financing, etc. Create them in a word processing program so they can be used as templates for later offers. This will save a lot of time down the road because an offer will not have to be written from scratch every time a new deal is in the works. Then, set a goal of writing a minimum number of proposals every week.

STEP 7: BUILD YOUR TEAM

Remember, real estate is a "team sport." A good network of contacts who can help an investor create deals and see them through is needed.

Right from the start, reach out to mortgage brokers, real estate lawyers, maintenance and repair individuals, etc. Introduce oneself, one's objectives, and make them aware of how they will benefit from working with an investor.

STEP 8: BECOME A REALTOR

As stated earlier, 80 to 90 percent of the real estate market is controlled by realtors, so take advantage of that fact and become licensed. This will provide access to comparables and to the network of realtors in the area. Be sure to get a realtor on the team if obtaining a license is unappealing.

STEP 9: ONGOING LEARNING AND REVIEW

Commit to learning something new about lease options, the local real estate market, the national economy, selling skills, financial skills, etc. every week. It can be as simple as reading newspaper articles or reading an entire book. It does not matter as long as learning is being done and staying up-to-date is accomplished. By staying current, an investor can spot opportunities faster than the competition and close deals quicker. In addition to learning, review goals on a monthly basis. Then, at the end of the year, do a comprehensive review and set new goals for the next year. Always, set and review goals. They keep a person on track and motivated. Remember, one of the universal characteristics of successful people is their ability to set goals, keep their eyes on those goals, and do everything they can, legally and morally, to achieve their aims. The motivational speaker and author of *The Psychology of Winning* Denis Waitley clearly defines the importance of goals:

> *"The reason most people never reach their goals is that they do not define them, or ever seriously consider them as believable or achievable. Winners can tell you where they are going, what they*

plan to do along the way, and who will be sharing the adventure with them."

STEP 10: LEAD A BALANCED LIFE

For those who have families and want to launch a career in lease options, it is important to remember the impact one's actions will have on loved ones. After all, business life directly affects personal relationships. That makes a balanced life an absolute necessity. Starting a new venture and pursuing it requires commitment, but does not require obsession with making money, beating out the competition at all costs, etc. Good, healthy personal relationships should be a top priority. Often, stress on relationships is not created by big events but small, cumulative ones like being disorganized, focusing too much on details instead of the big picture, etc. In other words, it is bad time management. For those planning to start out with lease options on a part-time basis, it is particularly important to have effective time management skills because a full-time job will be held down at the same time. There are many approaches to good time management, but at the core of each one, there are usually three central principles: analysis, planning, and commitment. The first principle, analysis, is simply finding out where one's time is currently going. This can be done in simple or complex form. For example, a basic approach is to simply review a selected week and see if time is being spent on activities that are leading directly to goals or if time is being wasted on unimportant or counter-productive activities. Those who are more disciplined and want to find out exactly where their time is going can keep a time log. This is a daily record of the activities being undertaken. For a month or more, use a planner to write down activities that take place during 15 minute or half-hour blocks. There is no denying a time log's effectiveness in pinpointing time management strengths and weaknesses; there is also no denying that few people can complete such a detailed time log. It is very difficult to track activities in such detail over a sustained period of time. Our advice: choose the system that best fits one's personality, work and personal life. Here are some general guidelines that can fit into any system:

- **Guideline 1: Make your major goals your first priority.** It makes sense to emphasize any goal that gets a lease option deal or increases the profitability on that deal. Common sense says that these important actions beat spending time shuffling paper or sharpening pencils. In other words, do not make the mistake many people make and confuse efficiency with effectiveness. As the management guru Peter Drucker said, "Efficiency is doing things the right way; effectiveness is doing the right things." Of course, it is important to do things efficiently because it saves time, money, and effort. But, often, we get so caught up in completing minor tasks the right way that we lose sight of the major tasks that will more immediately and effectively achieve our goals. Concentrate on tasks that lead directly to more deals and more profitability. An effective approach is to prioritize tasks on a daily basis. For example, at the beginning of the day or at the end of the previous day, list the tasks and assign them a numerical priority value: 1 = most important, 2 = important, 3 = can wait, 4 = not important ... etc.

- **Guideline 2: Try to do the most challenging work at your peak performance cycles.** Common sense says not to try to close an important deal when the investor and the customer are tired. Try to attend meetings, write difficult proposals, call on customers, etc. during a personal peak time in the day. This could be early morning, late morning, early afternoon — it all depends on biorhythms.

- **Guideline 3: Group similar activities together to maximize**

efficiency. Once we get into an activity, we gain rhythm and synergy. It makes sense to group them together into blocks. For example, spend a morning writing offers, block out a couple of hours for contacting customers, spend an afternoon doing research.

- **Guideline 4: Delegate.** Once the business grows, it may be necessary to take on employees. If this is the case, delegate responsibilities to those employees. Do not make the mistake of poor entrepreneurs who think they have to do it all. That is a recipe for burnout. Instead, hire employees to fill in gaps in one's knowledge and expertise and then let them do their jobs.

- **Guideline 5: Take breaks, get exercise.** Every body, every mind needs a break now and then. Tired minds make bad decisions and tired bodies contribute to those bad decisions. Think of mental and physical well being as a vital asset to one's success. The human mind craves variety, not only because it gets tired from doing the same thing over and over again, but because variety also contributes to creativity. The brain loves new ideas and techniques. Take breaks during the day and plan exercise periods on a regular basis. Choose a sport or hobby that suits one's personality — jog, swim, play tennis, do yoga, play chess, etc.

Finally, always keep the benefits of a balanced life and time management firmly in mind. They include:

- Accomplishment of more in less time

- Decreased frustration and anxiety

- Earning more money

- Increased personal productivity and achievement

- Increased joy and satisfaction

- More positive recognition

- More time for evaluation and planning

- More time for your family and friends

- More time for recreation

- Reduced stress

STEP 11: ESTABLISH A ROTH IRA

The Roth IRA (Individual Retirement Arrangement) is mainly an individual savings plan which can also be used as a source of funds for buying lease options. It was created by the Taxpayer Relief Act of 1997 and is named after Delaware Senator William V. Roth Jr. who advocated the idea of expanded IRAs. The Roth permits a person to allow one's capital to accumulate tax free under certain conditions. Individuals can invest up to $4,000 per year or $5,000 for those who are age 50 and over. Up to a specified limit, contributions can be made on a nondeductible basis. This means a person can make a contribution to his or her Roth IRA but not take a deduction on the income tax for the contribution as with a traditional IRA. Withdrawals are tax free within certain limitations. Any money earned by the Roth IRA is not taxed when a person makes a distribution within the conditions of distribution.

A Roth IRA must be set up with an IRS approved institution such as banks, some credit unions, brokerages, and so on. When setting up a

Roth IRA, a person will receive the IRA disclosure statement and the IRA adoption agreement and plan document. A Roth IRA can be established at anytime during the year, but contributions for a tax year must be made before the tax filing deadline. We recommend contacting an accountant, financial institution, or broker on setting up a program. Contributions can be made after age 70 ½ unlike the age limitation of a traditional IRA.

The Roth IRA has both advantages and disadvantages. Advantages include:

- Eligible individuals may contribute up to a specified limit annually.

- Contribution eligibility is not restricted by active participation in an employer's retirement plan.

- Withdrawals of earnings upon death or disability, for first time home buying, or after age 59 ½ are tax-free provided a five year wait has occurred.

Disadvantages include:

- Premature withdrawals in excess of contributions are fully taxable and are also subject to a ten percent penalty.

- Contributions are limited each year for each individual.

Maximum contributions limits are the lesser of the annual dollar limit of the table below or 100 percent of earned income less contributions to traditional IRAs.

The annual dollar limit is:

- 2006 ..... $4,000

- 2007 ..... $4,000

- 2008 ..... $5,000

For those 50 and over before the close of the taxable year, the following annual limit applies:

- 2006 ..... $5,000

- 2007 ..... $5,000

- 2008 ..... $6,000

After 2008, the contribution is to be adjusted for cost-of-living increases. Check for updates on Roth IRA requirements on the Internet at (**http://www.irs.gov/retirement/article/0,,id=137307,00.html**).

There are phase-out rules for the Roth IRA. If a person has an earned income or is the spouse of someone with an earned income, he or she might be able to contribute to a Roth IRA. If that earned income reaches a certain level, the amount that can be contributed to a Roth IRA is reduced or phased out all together. It is important to establish a Roth early in one's real estate career because once a person becomes successful in lease options, he or she will be making too much money. The income level where this phase-out occurs depends on one's income tax filing status. The phase-out rules for persons with a high earned income are as follows:

- **Single:** If one's income tax filing status is single, the Roth IRA contribution limit is reduced when the adjusted gross income is more than $95,000. The contribution limit is zero when the adjusted gross income reaches $110,000.

- **Married Filing Jointly:** Married persons filing jointly will have a reduced contribution limit for each person's Roth IRA if their adjusted gross income exceeds $150,000. If their adjusted gross income reaches $160,000, each person's contribution limit is zero.

- **Married filing separately and living apart:** If a person is married but files separately and has lived apart from his or her spouse for the entire tax year, the Roth IRA contribution amount will be reduced if the adjusted gross income is more than $95,000. The Roth IRA contribution limit will be eliminated if the adjusted gross income reaches $110,000.

- **Married filing separately and lived with spouse:** If a person is married, filing separately, and has lived with his or her spouse at any time during the tax year, the Roth IRA contribution amount will be reduced when the adjusted gross income exceeds $0.00 and will be completely eliminated when the adjusted gross income reaches $10,000.

If a person is not sure whether or not he or she can contribute to a Roth IRA, consult with a financial advisor or financial institution.

There are also distribution rules for the Roth. If a person has more than one Roth IRA, they are treated as a single account when calculating the tax consequences of distributions from any of them. To be tax-free, a distribution of earnings must meet both of the following requirements:

- The distribution must be made after the five year holding period.

- The distribution must be made on or after the individual reaches age 59 ½, made to the individuals beneficiary or estate, made to the individual who is become disabled, or made for a first time home purchase.

Contributions can be withdrawn at any time without penalty or tax.

STEP 12: FORM A LIMITED LIABILITY COMPANY (LLC)

This is a hybrid form of ownership that combines the properties of a corporation and partnership. If possible, form an LLC at the beginning of one's entry into the real estate market. Be sure to check with an attorney to find out what the regulations are in the state regarding LLCs and if one is appropriate for the situation. If so, an LLC has many advantages. First, it provides the flexibility and tax advantages of a partnership while maintaining the limited-liability benefits of a corporation. Like a corporation, an LLC is a separate legal entity that limits the liability of its members, but, unlike a corporation, it has the tax benefits of a partnership. Second, LLCs are free of many of the legal requirements that govern corporations, including annual reports, director meetings, shareholder requirements and so on. Third, LLCs are a pass through tax entity. This means company profits and losses are passed through the business and taxed solely on the members' individual tax returns. Fourth, once real estate holdings are grown, a person can partner with "members." The members can then hire a management group to run the LLC. This group can consist of members, nonmembers, or a combination. Fifth, members can split profits and losses any way they wish. Sixth, dividend distribution is nontaxable, unlike another form of incorporation — the "S" corporation — in which dividends are taxable. Seventh, an unlimited number of members may join a single LLC and most states allow single-member LLCs. Finally, an LLC may affiliate with other businesses, unlike an S corporation, where that ability is limited.

LLCs also have disadvantages. Costs can be greater. Some states impose income or franchise taxes on LLCs or require LLCs to pay annual fees to operate in that state. There is also a lack of legal precedent. Because LLCs have existed as legal business entities only since 1996, there is not a great deal of legal precedent available to help a person predict how legal disputes may affect a business. Every state has its own requirements. Check with an attorney who specializes in LLCs before deciding to form a limited liability corporation.

SAMPLE SWOT ANALYSIS FORM

Strengths	Weaknesses
Opportunities	Threats

CONCLUSION

This book has provided a hands-on, practical approach to building wealth in the area of lease options. As stated in the previous chapter, action is the key to success in the real estate market. Get started today on planning, goal setting, and analysis of personal strengths and weaknesses. Then, once a person has started, apply or develop the entrepreneurial attributes required to continue on the path to a secure financial future — optimism, patience, perseverance, ethical behavior, and a complete commitment for success.

Above all, commit to learning, not only now, but on a continuous basis. Learn from the best in the field on a local, regional, and national basis. Talk to other investors in the area. Tap into resources on the Internet and in books, seminars, workshops, CDs, and DVDs/videotapes. A person does not need to be a genius to succeed in lease options. As famed investor and philanthropist Warren Buffet said: "You don't need to be a rocket scientist. Investing is not a game where the guy with a 160 IQ beats the guy with a 130 IQ." However, it is key to be well informed. Knowledge provides the power to deal effectively and successfully with people, legal processes, finances, and the rules and regulations of the real estate market.

In a sense, the message at the heart of this entire book is not really about real estate at all. It is about taking control of one's life through lease options and other strategies. That is what all entrepreneurs do — take control of their lives. As many others have said, the world is full of talented, but poor people. They have squandered their talent by failing to take action and by letting others take control of their lives. Do not make the mistake of being passive and thinking, "Well, I will get into lease options someday." Instead, get active and get excited about the future in real estate.

Real estate — and any other form of entrepreneurship — is exciting. It offers so many possibilities and unlimited potential for not only building wealth, but a better version of oneself. True entrepreneurs marry their dreams to hard work. They shape their lives and the lives of those around them with dedication, commitment, and the ability to think big.

Here is a final piece of advice: Join the rank of big thinkers and create a life through lease options — a life of financial security, excitement, opportunity, and unlimited potential.

RESOURCES

I n addition to the print books listed below, the Internet is a rich source of articles, e-books, and other information on the topic of lease options and other areas of real estate. Use search engines to find real estate-related Web sites.

Carey, Chantal Howell & Bill Carey, *The New Path to Real Estate Wealth*, John Wiley & Sons, Copyright 2004

Chan, Matthew S., *Turnkey Investing with Lease Options*, Ascend Beyond Publishing, Copyright 2004

Irwin, Robert, *How to Get Started in Real Estate Investing, American Media International*, Copyright 2003

Keller, Gary, Jenks, Dave and Papasan, Jay, *The Millionaire Real Estate Investor*, McGraw-Hill, Copyright 2005

Kiyosaki, Robert T., with Sharon L. Lechter, *Rich Dad, Poor Dad*, Warner Books in association with CASHFLOW Technologies, Inc., Copyright 1997,1998

Lucier, Thomas J, *How to Make Money with Real Estate Options*, John Wiley & Sons, Copyright 2005

Patton, Wendy, *Investing in Real Estate with Lease Options and "Subject-To" Deals*, John Wiley & Sons, Copyright 2005

Robinson, Leigh, *Landlording*, ExPress, Ninth Edition, Copyright 2004

Shemin, Robert, *Secrets of a Millionaire Landlord*, Dearborn Financial Publishing, Inc., Copyright 2002

AUTHOR BIOGRAPHY

Steven D. Fisher is an independent writer, illustrator, and instructional designer with over 25 years of experience in the fields of business writing and training and development. His specialties include the design and writing of books, certification tests, e-Books, manuals, seminars and workshops. In addition to practical "real world" experience, he holds an M.A. in Education of the Hearing Impaired and trained as a print and media Broadcast Specialist in the U.S. Army.

GLOSSARY

Abatement Sometimes referred to as free rent or early occupancy. A condition that could happen in addition to the primary term of the lease.

Absorption Rate The speed and amount of time at which rentable space, in square feet, is filled.

Abstract or Title Search The process of reviewing all transactions that have been recorded publicly in order to determine whether any defects in the title exist that could interfere with a clear property ownership transfer.

Accelerated Depreciation A method of depreciation where the value of a property depreciates faster in the first few years after purchasing it.

Acceptance The seller's written approval of a buyer's offer.

Addendum An addition or update for an existing contract between parties.

Additional Principal Payment Additional money paid to the lender, apart from the scheduled loan payments, to pay more of the principal balance, shortening the length of the loan.

Adjusted Funds From Operations (AFFO) The rate of REIT performance or ability to pay dividends that is used by many analysts who have concerns about the quality of earnings as measured by Funds From Operations (FFO).

Administrative Fee A percentage of the value of the assets under management, or a fixed annual dollar amount charged to manage an account.

Adviser A broker or investment banker who represents an owner in a transaction and is paid a retainer and/or a performance fee once a financing or sales transaction has closed.

Agency Closing A type of closing in which a lender uses a title company or other firm as an agent to finish a loan.

Agency Disclosure A requirement in most states that agents who act for both buyers or sellers must disclose who they are working for in the transaction.

Agreement of Sale A legal document the buyer and seller must approve and sign that details the price and terms in the transaction.

Annual Percentage Rate (APR) The interest rate that states the actual cost of borrowing money over the course of a year.

Application The form a borrower must complete in order to apply for a mortgage loan, including information such as income, savings, assets, and debts.

Application Fee A fee some lenders charge that may include charges for items such as property appraisal or a credit report unless those fees are included elsewhere.

Appraisal The estimate of the value of a property on a particular date given by a professional appraiser, usually presented in a written document.

Appraisal Fee The fee charged by a professional appraiser for his estimate of the market value of a property.

Appraisal Report The written report presented by an appraiser regarding the value of a property.

Appraised Value The dollar amount a professional appraiser assigned to the value of a property in his report.

Appraiser A certified individual who is qualified by education, training, and experience to estimate the value of real and personal property.

Appreciation An increase in the home's or property's value.

Appreciation Return The amount gained when the value of the real estate assets increases during the current quarter.

As-Is Condition A phrase in a purchase or lease contract in which the new tenant accepts the existing condition of the premises as well as any physical defects.

Assessed Value The value placed on a home that is determined by a tax assessor in order to calculate a tax base.

Assessment (1) The approximate value of a property. (2) A fee charged in addition to taxes in order to help pay for items such as water, sewer, street improvements, etc.

Assessor A public officer who estimates the value of a property for the purpose of taxation.

Assignment The transfer of rights and responsibilities from one party to another for paying a debt. The original party remains liable for the debt should the second party default.

Assignor The person who transfers the rights and interests of a property to another.

Assumable Mortgage A mortgage that is capable of being transferred to a different borrower.

Assumption The act of assuming the mortgage of the seller.

Assumption Clause A contractual provision that enables the buyer to take responsibility for the mortgage loan from the seller.

Assumption Fee A fee charged to the buyer for processing new records when they are assuming an existing loan.

Attorn To agree to recognize a new owner of a property and to pay rent to the new landlord.

Average Free Rent The number of months the rent abatement concession is expected to be granted to a tenant as part of an incentive to lease under current market conditions.

Average Occupancy The average rate of each of the previous 12 months that a property was occupied.

Average Total Assets The sum of the total assets of a company for the previous five quarters divided by five.

Bankrupt The state an individual or business is in if they are unable to repay their debt when it is due.

Bankruptcy A legal proceeding where a debtor can obtain relief from payment of certain obligations through restructuring their finances.

Base Rent A certain amount that is used as a minimum rent, providing for rent increases over the term of the lease agreement.

Before-Tax Income An individual's income before taxes have been deducted.

Break-Even Point The point at which a landlord's income from rent matches expenses and debt.

Bridge Loan A short-term loan for individuals or companies that are still seeking more permanent financing.

Broker A person who serves as a go-between for a buyer and seller.

Brokerage The process of bringing two or more parties together in exchange for a fee, commission, or other compensation.

Buildable Acres The portion of land that can be built on after allowances for roads, setbacks, anticipated open spaces, and unsuitable areas have been made.

Building Code The laws set forth by the local government regarding end use of a given piece of property. These law codes may dictate the design, materials used, and/or types of improvements that will be allowed.

Building Standard Plus Allowance A detailed list provided by the landlord stating the standard building materials and costs necessary to make the premises inhabitable.

Build-Out Improvements to a property's space that have been implemented according to the tenant's specifications.

Buydown Mortgage A style of home loan in which the lender receives a higher payment in order to convince them to reduce the interest rate during the initial years of the mortgage.

Capital Gain The amount of excess when the net proceeds from the sale of an asset are higher than its book value.

Capital Improvements Expenses that prolong the life of a property or add new improvements to it.

Capital Markets Public and private markets where individuals or businesses can raise or borrow capital.

Capitalization The mathematical process that investors use to derive the value of a property using the rate of return on investments.

Cash Flow The amount of income an investor receives on a rental property after operating expenses and loan payments have been deducted.

Cashier's Check A check the bank draws on its own resources instead of a depositor's account.

Certificate of Occupancy (CO) A written document issued by a local government or building agency that states that a home or other building is inhabitable after meeting all building codes.

Certificate of Reasonable Value (CRV) An appraisal presented by the Department of Veterans Affairs that shows the current market value of a property.

Certificate of Veteran Status A document veterans or reservists receive if they have served 90 days of continuous active duty (including training time).

Chain of Title The official record of all transfers of ownership over the history of a piece of property.

Class A A property rating that is usually assigned to those that will generate the maximum rent per square foot, due to superior quality and/or location.

Class B A good property that most potential tenants would find desirable but lacks certain attributes that would bring in the top dollar.

Class C A building that is physically acceptable but offers few amenities, thereby becoming cost-effective space for tenants who are seeking a particular image.

Clear Title A property title that is free of liens, defects, or other legal encumbrances.

Closing The final act of procuring a loan and title in which documents are signed between the buyer and seller and/or their respective representation and all money concerned in the contract changes hands.

Closing Costs The expenses that are related to the sale of real estate including loan, title, and appraisal fees and are beyond the price of the property itself.

Closing Statement See: Settlement Statement.

Collateralized Mortgage Obligation (CMO) Debt that is fully based on a pool of mortgages.

Co-Borrower Another individual who is jointly responsible for the loan and is on the title to the property.

Cost of Funds Index (COFI) An index used to determine changes in the interest rates for certain ARMs.

Co-Investment Program A separate account for an insurance company or investment partnership in which two or more pension funds may co-invest their capital in an individual property or a portfolio of properties.

Co-Investment The condition that occurs when two or more pension funds or groups of funds are sharing ownership of a real estate investment.

Collateral The property for which

a borrower has obtained a loan, thereby assuming the risk of losing the property if the loan is not repaid according to the terms of the loan agreement.

Collection The effort on the part of a lender, due to a borrower defaulting on a loan, which involves mailing and recording certain documents in the event that the foreclosure procedure must be implemented.

Commission A compensation to salespeople that is paid out of the total amount of the purchase transaction.

Commitment The agreement of a lender to make a loan with given terms for a specific period.

Commitment Fee The fee a lender charges for the guarantee of specified loan terms, to be honored at some point in the future.

Common Area Assessments Sometimes called Homeowners' Association Fees. Charges paid to the homeowners' association by the individual unit owners, in a condominium or planned unit development (PUD), that are usually used to maintain the property and common areas.

Common Area Maintenance The additional charges the tenant

must pay in addition to the base rent to pay for the maintenance of common areas.

Condemnation A government agency's act of taking private property, without the owner's consent, for public use through the power of eminent domain.

Conditional Commitment A lender's agreement to make a loan providing the borrower meets certain conditions.

Conditional Sale A contract to sell a property that states that the seller will retain the title until all contractual conditions have been fulfilled.

Condominium A type of ownership in which all of the unit owners own the property, common areas, and buildings jointly, and have sole ownership in the unit to which they hold the title.

Condominium Conversion Changing an existing rental property's ownership to the condominium form of ownership.

Condominium Hotel A condominium project that involves registration desks, short-term occupancy, food and telephone services, and daily cleaning services, and is generally operated as a commercial hotel even though the units are individually owned.

Conforming Loan A type of mortgage that meets the conditions to be purchased by Fannie Mae or Freddie Mac.

Construction Documents The drawings and specifications an architect and/or engineer provides to describe construction requirements for a project.

Consultant Any individual or company that provides the services to institutional investors, such as defining real estate investment policies, making recommendations to advisers or managers, analyzing existing real estate portfolios, monitoring and reporting on portfolio performance, and/or reviewing specified investment opportunities.

Consumer Price Index (CPI) A measurement of inflation, relating to the change in the prices of goods and services that are regularly purchased by a specific population during a certain period of time.

Contingency A specific condition that must be met before either party in a contract can be legally bound.

Contract An agreement, either verbal or written, to perform or not to perform a certain thing.

Contract Rent Also known as Face Rent. The dollar amount of the rental obligation specified in a lease.

Conventional Loan A long-term loan from a non-governmental lender that a borrower obtains for the purchase of a home.

Conveyance The act of transferring a property title between parties by deed.

Cooperative Also called a Co-op. A type of ownership by multiple residents of a multi-unit housing complex in which they all own shares in the cooperative corporation that owns the property, thereby having the right to occupy a particular apartment or unit.

Cost-of-Sale Percentage An estimate of the expenses of selling an investment that represents brokerage commissions, closing costs, fees, and other necessary sales costs.

Credit An agreement in which a borrower promises to repay the lender at a later date and receives something of value in exchange.

Credit History An individual's record which details his current and past financial obligations and performance.

Credit Rating The degree of creditworthiness a person is assigned based on his credit history and current financial status.

Credit Report A record detailing an individual's credit, employment, and residence history used to determine the individual's creditworthiness.

Credit Score Sometimes called a Credit Risk Score. The number contained in a consumer's credit report that represents a statistical summary of the information.

Creditor A party to whom other parties owe money.

Current Occupancy The current percentage of units in a building or property that is leased.

Debt Any amount one party owes to another party.

Debt-to-Income Ratio The percentage of a borrower's monthly payment on long-term debts divided by his gross monthly income.

Deed A legal document that conveys property ownership to the buyer.

Delinquency A state that occurs when the borrower fails to make mortgage payments on time, eventually resulting in foreclosure, if severe enough.

Delinquent Mortgage A mortgage in which the borrower is behind on payments.

Demising Wall The physical partition between the spaces of two tenants or from the building's common areas.

Deposit Also referred to as Earnest Money. The funds that the buyer provides when offering to purchase property.

Depreciation A decline in the value of property or an asset, often used as a tax-deductible item.

Disclosure A written statement, presented to a potential buyer, that lists information relevant to a piece of property, whether positive or negative.

Down Payment The variance between the purchase price and the portion that the mortgage lender financed.

Earthquake Insurance A type of insurance policy that provides coverage against earthquake damage to a home.

Easement The right given to a non-ownership party to use a certain part of the property for specified purposes, such as servicing power lines or cable lines.

Economic Feasibility The viability of a building or project in terms of costs and revenue where the degree of viability is established by extra revenue.

Economic Rent The market rental value of a property at a particular point in time.

Effective Rent The actual rental rate that the landlord achieves after deducting the concession value from the base rental rate a tenant pays.

Entitlement A benefit of a VA home loan. Often referred to as Eligibility.

Equal Credit Opportunity Act (ECOA) A federal law that requires a lender or other creditor to make credit available for applicants regardless of sex, marital status, race, religion, or age.

Equifax One of the three primary credit-reporting bureaus.

Equity The value of a property after existing liabilities have been deducted.

Estate The total assets, including property, of an individual after he has died.

Estimated Hazard Insurance An estimation of hazard insurance, or homeowner's insurance, that will cover physical risks.

Estimated Property Taxes An estimation of the property taxes that must be paid on the property, according to state and county tax rates.

Examination of Title A title company's inspection and report of public records and other documents for the purpose of determining the chain of ownership of a property.

Exclusive Agency Listing A written agreement between a property owner and a real estate broker in which the owner promises to pay the broker a commission if certain property is leased during the listing period.

Exclusive Listing A contract that allows a licensed real estate agent to be the only agent who can sell a property for a given time.

Experian One of the three primary credit-reporting bureaus.

Face Rental Rate The rental rate that the landlord publishes.

Fair Credit Reporting Act (FCRA) The federal legislation that governs the processes credit reporting agencies must follow.

Fair Housing Act The federal legislation that prohibits the refusal to rent or sell to anyone based on race, color, religion, sex, family status, or disability.

Fair Market Value The highest price that a buyer would be willing to pay, and the lowest a seller would be willing to accept.

Federal Housing Administration (FHA) A government agency that provides low-rate mortgages to buyers who are able to make a down payment as low as 3 percent.

Fixed Costs Expenses that remain the same despite the level of sales or production.

Flood Insurance A policy that is required in designated flood zones to protect against loss due to flood damage.

Floor Area Ratio (FAR) A measurement of a building's gross square footage compared to the square footage of the land on which it is located.

For Sale By Owner (FSBO) A method of selling property in which the property owner serves as the selling agent and directly handles the sales process with the buyer or buyer's agent.

Foreclosure The legal process in which a lender takes over ownership of a property once the borrower is in default in a mortgage arrangement.

Front-End Ratio The measurement a lender uses to compare a borrower's monthly housing expense to gross monthly income.

Full-Service Rent A rental rate that includes all operating expenses and real estate taxes for the first year.

Hazard Insurance Also known as Homeowner's Insurance or Fire Insurance. A policy that provides coverage for damage from forces such as fire and wind.

Hold-Over Tenant A tenant who retains possession of the leased premises after the lease has expired.

Home Equity Loan A type of loan that allows owners to borrow against the equity in their homes up to a limited amount.

Home Inspection A pre-purchase examination of the condition a home is in by a certified inspector.

Home Inspector A certified professional who determines the structural soundness and operating systems of a property.

Home Price The price that a buyer and seller agree upon, generally based on the home's appraised market value.

Homeowners' Association (HOA) A group that governs a community, condominium building, or neighborhood and enforces the covenants, conditions, and restrictions set by the developer.

Homeowners' Association Dues The monthly payments that are paid to the homeowners' association for maintenance and communal expenses.

Homeowner's Insurance A policy that includes coverage for all damages that may affect the value of a house as defined in the terms of the insurance policy.

Improvements The upgrades or changes made to a building to improve its value or usefulness.

Incentive Fee A structure in which the fee amount charged is based on the performance of the real estate assets under management.

Inspection Fee The fee that a licensed property inspector charges for determining the current physical condition of the property.

Inspection Report A written report of the property's condition presented by a licensed inspection professional.

Joint Tenancy A form of ownership in which two or more people have equal shares in a piece of property, and rights pass to the surviving owner(s) in the event of death.

Lease Option A financing option that provides for homebuyers to lease a home with an option to buy, with part of the rental payments being applied toward the down payment.

Lender A bank or other financial institution that offers home loans.

Liabilities Borrower's debts and financial obligations, whether long- or short-term.

Liability Insurance A type of policy that protects owners against negligence, personal injury, or property damage claims.

Listing Agreement An agreement between a property owner and a real estate broker that authorizes the broker to attempt to sell or lease the property at a specified price and terms in return for a commission or other compensation.

Loan An amount of money that is borrowed and usually repaid with interest.

Monthly Association Dues A payment due each month to a homeowners' association for expenses relating to maintenance and community operations.

Mortgage An amount of money that is borrowed to purchase a property using that property as collateral.

Mortgage Banker A financial institution that provides home loans using its own resources, often selling them to investors such as insurance companies or Fannie Mae.

Mortgage Broker An individual

who matches prospective borrowers with lenders that the broker is approved to deal with.

Mortgage Broker Business A company that matches prospective borrowers with lenders that the broker is approved to deal with.

Mortgage Insurance (MI) A policy, required by lenders on some loans, that covers the lender against certain losses that are incurred as a result of a default on a home loan.

Mortgage Insurance Premium (MIP) The amount charged for mortgage insurance, either to a government agency or to a private MI company.

Mortgage Life and Disability Insurance A type of term life insurance borrowers often purchase to cover debt that is left when the borrower dies or becomes too disabled to make the mortgage payments.

Mortgagee The financial institution that lends money to the borrower.

Mortgagor The person who requests to borrow money to purchase a property.

Multi-Dwelling Units A set of properties that provide separate housing areas for more than one family but only require a single mortgage.

Net Operating Income (NOI) The pre-tax figure of gross revenue minus operating expenses and an allowance for expected vacancy.

Offer A term that describes a specified price or spread to sell whole loans or securities.

Operating Cost Escalation A clause that is intended to adjust rents to account for external standards such as published indexes, negotiated wage levels, or building-related expenses.

Operating Expense The regular costs associated with operating and managing a property.

Opportunistic A phrase that generally describes a strategy of holding investments in under-performing and/or under-managed assets with the expectation of increases in cash flow and/or value.

Option A condition in which the buyer pays for the right to purchase a property within a certain period of time without the obligation to buy.

Owner Financing A transaction in which the property seller agrees to finance all or part of the amount of the purchase.

Performance Measurement The process of measuring how well an investor's real estate has performed regarding individual assets, advisers/

managers, and portfolios.

Pre-Leased A certain amount of space in a proposed building that must be leased before construction may begin or a certificate of occupancy may be issued.

Price-to-Earnings Ratio The comparison that is derived by dividing the current share price by the sum of the primary earnings per share from continuing operations over the past year.

Primary Issuance The preliminary financing of an issuer.

Prime Tenant The largest or highest-earning tenant in a building or shopping center.

Property Tax The tax that must be paid on private property.

Purchase Agreement The written contract the buyer and seller both sign defining the terms and conditions under which a property is sold.

Real Estate Agent An individual who is licensed to negotiate and transact the real estate sales.

Real Estate Fundamentals The factors that drive the value of property.

Real Property Land and anything else of a permanent nature that is affixed to the land.

Realtor A real estate agent or broker who is an active member of a local real estate board affiliated with the National Association of Realtors.

Recorder A public official who records transactions that affect real estate in the area.

Recording The documentation that the registrar's office keeps of the details of properly executed legal documents.

Recording Fee A fee real estate agents charge for moving the sale of a piece of property into the public record.

Renewal Option A clause in a lease agreement that allows a tenant to extend the term of a lease.

Renewal Probability The average percentage of a building's tenants who are expected to renew terms at market rental rates upon the lease expiration.

Rent Commencement Date The date at which a tenant is to begin paying rent.

Rent Loss Insurance A policy that covers loss of rent or rental value for a landlord due to any condition that renders the leased premises inhabitable, thereby excusing the tenant from paying rent.

Rent The fee paid for the occupancy and/or use of any rental property or equipment.

Rentable/Usable Ratio A total rentable area in a building divided by the area available for use.

Rental Growth Rate The projected trend of market rental rates over a particular period of analysis.

Rent-Up Period The period of time following completion of a new building when tenants are actively being sought and the project is stabilizing.

Return on Equity The measurement of the return on the investment in a business or property.

Return on Investments The percentage of money that has been gained as a result of certain investments.

Reverse Mortgage See: Home Equity Conversion Mortgage.

Revenue per Available Room (RevPAR) The total room revenue for a particular period divided by the average number of rooms available in a hospitality facility.

Risk Management A logical approach to analyzing and defining

insurable and non-insurable risks while evaluating the availability and costs of purchasing third-party insurance.

Roll-Over Risk The possibility that tenants will not renew their lease.

Sale-Leaseback An arrangement in which a seller deeds a property, or part of it, to a buyer in exchange for money or the equivalent, then leases the property from the new owner.

Sales Comparison Value A value that is calculated by comparing the appraised property to similar properties in the area that have been recently sold.

Seller Financing A type of funding in which the borrower may use part of the equity in the property to finance the purchase.

Settlement or Closing Fees The fees that the escrow agent receives for carrying out the written instructions in the agreement between borrower and lender and/or buyer and seller.

Stabilized Occupancy The best projected range of long-term occupancy that a piece of rental property will achieve after existing in the open market for a reasonable period of time with terms and conditions that are comparable to similar offerings.

Subdivision The most common type of housing development created by dividing a larger tract of land into individual lots for sale or lease.

Sublessee A person or business that holds the rights of use and occupancy under a lease contract with the original lessee, who still retains primary responsibility for the lease obligations.

Survey A document or analysis containing the precise measurements of a piece of property as performed by a licensed surveyor.

Tenancy by the Entirety A form of ownership held by spouses in which they both hold title to the entire property with right of survivorship.

Tenancy in Common A type of ownership held by two or more owners in an undivided interest in the property with no right of survivorship.

Tenant (Lessee) A party who rents a piece of real estate from another by way of a lease agreement.

Tenant at Will A person who possesses a piece of real estate with the owner's permission.

Tenant Improvement (TI) Allowance The specified amount of money that the landlord contributes toward tenant improvements.

Tenant Improvement (TI) The upgrades or repairs that are made to the leased premises by or for a tenant.

Title The legal written document that provides someone ownership in a piece of real estate.

Title Search The process of analyzing all transactions existing in the public record in order to determine whether any title defects could interfere with the clear transfer of property ownership.

Total Acres The complete amount of land area that is contained within a real estate investment.

Total Expense Ratio The comparison of monthly debt obligations to gross monthly income.

Total Inventory The total amount of square footage commanded by property within a geographical area.

Total Monthly Housing Costs The amount that must be paid each month to cover principal, interest, property taxes, PMI, and/or either hazard insurance or homeowners' association dues.

Total Return The final amount of income and appreciation returns per quarter.

Townhouse An attached home that is not considered to be a condominium.

TransUnion Corporation One of the primary credit-reporting bureaus.

Transfer Tax An amount specified by state or local authorities when ownership in a piece of property changes hands.

Triple Net Lease A lease that requires the tenant to pay all property expenses on top of the rental payments.

Two- to Four-Family Property A structure that provides living space for two to four families while ownership is held in a single deed.

Usable Square Footage The total area that is included within the exterior walls of the tenant's space.

Use The particular purpose for which a property is intended to be employed.

Vacancy Factor The percentage of gross revenue that pro-forma income statements expect to be lost due to vacancies.

Vacancy Rate The percentage of space that is available to rent.

Vacant Space Existing rental space that is presently being marketed for lease minus space that is available for sublease.

Variance A permission that enables a property owner to work around a zoning ordinance's literal requirements which cause a unique hardship due to special circumstances.

Verification of Employment (VOE) The confirmation statement a borrower's employer may be asked to sign in order to verify the borrower's position and salary.

Write-Off A procedure used in accounting when an asset is determined to be uncollectible and is therefore considered to be a loss.

Zoning Ordinance The regulations and laws that control the use or improvement of land in a particular area or zone.

Zoning The act of dividing a city or town into particular areas and applying laws and regulations regarding the architectural design, structure, and intended uses of buildings within those areas.

INDEX

1031 Tax-Deferred Exchange law 85

A
American Prepaid Legal Services Institute 245
Appraiser 44, 67, 80, 100, 102, 205, 206, 213, 214

B
Bird dog 76
Boot 93, 94, 95, 96
Bronchick, William 167
Building permits 43, 44, 45
Bureau of Labor Statistics 41, 248, 249

C
Canceled checks 29
Certified mail 165

Chan, Matthew 271
Checks, canceled 30
Classified ads 177
Computer age 197
Computer applications 33, 197
Cosmetic changes 56
County property appraiser 80, 100, 102
Credit bureau 27, 29
Credit card 27, 30, 31, 33, 72, 159
Creditor 27, 28, 50
Credit rating 25, 26, 29, 208, 233
Credit report 25, 26, 27, 28, 29, 31, 159

D
Debtor-creditor relationship 50
Department of Housing and Urban Development (HUD) deed 101, 192
Detroit 42

Discrimination 159, 161, 234
Driver's license 32
Duplexes 220, 221, 224

E

Eminent domain 135, 138, 188
Entry right 134
Environmental hazards 100, 101,
    102, 194
Equity skimming 50
Escrow 70, 94, 95, 120, 134, 136,
    141, 142, 143, 147, 148,
    179, 185, 186, 191
Eviction process 165, 168

F

"For Sale by Owner" 78
Fair Housing Act of 1968 160
Financial education 33
First mortgage 79, 119, 189
Flood zone 100
Foreclosure 48, 73, 148, 187
Fraud 31, 105
Functional obsolescence 56

G

Goal 3, 8, 9, 11, 19, 20, 21, 22,
    23, 33, 37, 73, 76, 83, 117,
    237, 240, 259, 261, 269

H

Hazardous waste 100
Home builder 16
Home equity line of credit 72

How to Make Money with Real
    Estate Options, 50, 78, 271

I

Identity theft 30, 31
Internet ads 76
Investing in Real Estate with Lease
    Options and "Subject-To"
    Deals 149, 272
Investor 2, 34, 46, 65, 149, 271

J

Job growth 41
Job outsourcing 42

L

Landlord 45, 49, 52, 86, 119, 159,
    160, 162, 165, 167, 168,
    169, 170, 215, 217, 218,
    220, 222, 223, 225, 226,
    232, 233, 234, 235, 236,
    237, 238, 240, 241, 242,
    243, 244, 245, 248, 250,
    253
Lease agreement 52, 53
Lease option 1, 2, 3, 4, 8, 11, 16,
    17, 21, 22, 23, 33, 39, 40,
    48, 49, 50, 51, 55, 58, 59,
    60, 65, 66, 77, 78, 81, 82,
    83, 84, 85, 87, 88, 89, 90,
    99, 105, 106, 111, 117, 118,
    119, 120, 124, 128, 129,
    131, 133, 135, 136, 142,
    148, 150, 157, 159, 163,
    164, 166, 174, 175, 197,

211, 218, 219, 256, 259, 261

Lender 17, 18, 49, 50, 54, 67, 71, 72, 95, 206, 208, 209, 247

liability insurance certificate 157

Lien 103, 104, 138, 148, 157, 158

Local market 10

Local market 18, 37, 38, 39, 59, 133

Lucier, Thomas J 271

M

Management company 35, 252

Marketable title 139, 151, 154

Memorandum of option 4, 142, 147, 148

Microsoft Excel 33

Minimum wage workers 42

Mobile homes 219

Monthly statements 30

Mortgage broker 18, 208

Mortgage loan 17, 189

MYOB Accounting 198

N

Neal Patricia 9

Negotiation 117, 127

Notice of Assignment 179

Notice of Exercise of Real Estate Option letter 185

Notices to vacate 167, 169, 189

O

Obsolescent properties 55, 57, 58

Occupancy rate 45

Option credits 119

P

Path of progress 39, 46, 47, 57, 59, 71, 173, 214

Patton, Wendy 149, 151, 153, 272

Peachtree Accounting 198

Pets 169, 220, 232, 234

PIN number 30

Plumbing 114, 116, 215, 244

Police report 31

Promissory note 94, 194

Property management software 34, 198

Property tax value 67

Property values 2, 39, 40, 67, 68, 69

Public hearings 60

Q

QuickBooks 33, 198, 240

Quicken 33

R

Real estate broker 209

Real estate developers 16

Real estate investment clubs 80

Rental guides 224

Rental Property Tracker Plus 240

Rent levels 46

RentTracker 240

Renttracker 240

Request for Investigation 26, 27

Rezoning application 60, 61, 63

S

School systems 39
Seattle 42, 161
Signage 223
Single residence occupancy
    buildings 219
Survey 112, 194

T

Tax advisor 96, 206, 207
Tax identification numbers 102
Team development 200
Tenant-buyer 48, 49, 50
Termite/pest control inspection
    report 194
Testimonials 83, 130, 258
The Real Estate Investor's
    Handbook 2, 34, 46

Title search 102, 105
Transfer fees 119
Turnkey Investing with Lease-
    Options 3, 165

U

Unconditional quit notices 169

W

Web site 32, 175, 176, 177, 192,
    198
Woods, Tiger 10

Z

Zoning authority 60